Cake

hamlyn

Cake

80 classic & contemporary recipes

Joanna Farrow

Notes

Both metric and imperial measurements have been given in all recipes. Use one set of measurements only, and not a mixture of both.

Standard level spoon measurements are used in all recipes.
1 tablespoon = one 15 ml spoon
1 teaspoon = one 5 ml spoon

The Department of Health advises that eggs should not be consumed raw. This book contains dishes made with raw or lightly cooked eggs. It is prudent for vulnerable people such as pregnant and nursing mothers, invalids, the elderly, babies and young children to avoid uncooked or lightly cooked dishes made with eggs. Once prepared, these dishes should be kept refrigerated and used promptly.

This book includes dishes made with nuts and nut derivatives. It is advisable for those with known allergic reactions to nuts and nut derivatives and those who may be potentially vulnerable to these allergies, such as pregnant and nursing mothers, invalids, the elderly, babies and children, to avoid dishes made with nuts and nut oils. It is also prudent to check the labels of pre-prepared ingredients for the possible inclusion of nut derivatives.

Ovens should be preheated to the specified temperature. If using a fan-assisted oven, follow the manufacturer's instructions for adjusting the time and the temperature.

First published in Great Britain in 2007 by Hamlyn,
a division of Octopus Publishing Group Ltd
2–4 Heron Quays, London E14 4JP

ISBN-13: 978-0-600-61511-8
ISBN-10: 0-600-61511-1

A CIP catalogue record for this book is available from the British Library.

Printed and bound in China

10 9 8 7 6 5 4 3 2 1

Contents

Introduction *A piece of cake, accompanied by a cup of coffee or tea, is one of everyone's favourite comfort foods. Sweet and indulgent, it fills that little gap between meals, and it's a treat that's raised to new heights when the cake is freshly homemade from the best ingredients.*

This book aims to encourage cooks to get hooked on baking, to enjoy the therapeutic process of mixing and blending, to savour the wonderful smells as a cake bakes and, above all, to relish the appreciative murmurs of eager tasters.

The recipes are all easy to make and range from firm favourites to slightly quirkier creations for confirmed 'cake-aholics'. Some are best served absolutely fresh, preferably still slightly warm, while others are good keepers, perfect for feeding a crowd. And when you are stuck for something to take when visiting friends or family, what could be better than presenting them with one of your freshly baked creations?

Essential ingredients

Fats

Unsalted butter is used in the recipes in
this book because it imparts a good flavour
and is free from the additives that many
other adulterated spreads and margarines
contain, even if the pack specifies that they
can be used for baking. If you are short of
unsalted butter, the quantity can be topped
up or substituted with lightly salted butter,
but avoid using ordinary salted butter
because the salty flavour will affect the taste
of the cake.

Margarines and non-dairy spreads can be
used if necessary, but check that they are
suitable for baking before you buy. A
couple of the recipes use olive oil as an
alternative to butter. Choose an oil with a
mild or medium flavour so that it doesn't
dominate the other ingredients.

Sugar

Well-flavoured sugars, such as dark and light
muscovado and molasses sugar, impart
plenty of extra flavour to cakes and combine
well with chocolate, spices and treacle.
Occasionally, muscovado sugar hardens
during storage. To make it possible to cook
with, pop the pack in the microwave and
give it short bursts of medium power until
the sugar has softened. Most of the recipes
use unrefined golden caster sugar rather than
white sugar, unless the white colour is
essential for the appearance of the cake.

Eggs

For best colour and taste use good quality,
well-flavoured eggs. If you store eggs in the
refrigerator, try to remember to remove
them well before baking, because they will
give more volume and are less likely to
curdle in creamed mixtures when they are
at room temperature.

Flour

Self-raising flour is the type of flour most
widely used in cake making, because it
already includes a raising agent. Some
self-raising flours are sold specially for cake
baking – they are sifted more finely and are
designed to give a lighter sponge. A few
recipes in this book substitute wholemeal
flour for some of the quantity of white
flour, in order to give a more textured,
wholesome flavour. If you prefer wholemeal
flour, you can use it in any recipe as a
substitute for some of the white flour, but
avoid using wholemeal flour alone because
it tends to make a heavier cake.

Special equipment

You will probably already have most of the equipment you need to make most basic cakes, but the following items are essential.

Whisks

An electric whisk takes all the effort out of cake making. A free-standing, table-top model with whisk and beater attachments is very handy if you make a lot of cakes, particularly if you are working with larger quantities of ingredients. Use the beater for creamed mixtures and the whisk for fatless sponges and Genoese cakes. (You won't be able to position the bowl of a free-standing electric whisk over hot water to speed up the whisking process, but heating the bowl first may help.)

A large-capacity food processor is good for creamed mixtures, and a small, hand-held electric whisk is a useful all-round piece of equipment and cheaper than the above. Balloon whisks and rotary whisks can be used for any cakes, but the job will take a bit longer and be much harder work!

Cake tins

Strong, sturdy, deep cake tins will last for years so it's worth investing in a couple of sizes if you intend to do lots of baking. The most frequently used tins in this book are 18 cm (7 inch) and 20 cm (8 inch) round tins. Square tins can easily be substituted, but always use a slightly smaller size – for example, use a 15 cm (6 inch) square

instead of an 18 cm (7 inch) round, or an 18 cm (7 inch) square instead of a 20 cm (8 inch) round. A slightly larger tin can be used if you don't have the required size (the cake will be slightly shallower and the required cooking time might be slightly less), but don't squeeze a mixture into a smaller tin if you don't have the right size because it might spill over during baking or sink in the centre.

Most cake tins are available with a loose base, which makes it easier to remove the cake from the tin. A tin with a loose base is best for recipes that have a soft fruity or crumbly topping, which might get damaged if the cake were inverted. Rest the tin on a sturdy can or container and carefully pull down the tin sides to remove. Spring-form (or spring-release) tins are a good alternative because they can be easily unclipped and lifted away.

Muffin trays, sandwich tins, shallow rectangular tins and loaf tins are also useful for baking. Nonstick versions are widely available and tend to be harder wearing as they are not prone to rust. Before baking, line tins with greaseproof paper if the recipe requires it (see opposite). Lining nonstick tins is not essential, but does make the cakes easier to remove.

Silicone rubber flexible moulds are now available for small cakes, but they come in a more limited range of sizes. There's no need to grease the moulds, and the baked cakes can be easily popped out of them.

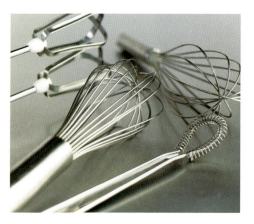

Lining cake tins

To line cake tins use greaseproof paper (or baking parchment if you haven't any greaseproof paper), and brush the tin's interior base and sides with melted butter before you start lining. Most cakes need a completely lined tin – that is, with both base and sides lined with paper – but others need only the base lined with a circle of paper. See the individual recipes for instructions about how the tins should be lined in each case.

Round tins

Using the tin as a guide, draw a circle on the greaseproof paper and cut it out. Cut strips of paper a little wider than the height of the tin, fold over a lip approximately 1 cm (½ inch) wide and snip it at intervals. Brush the sides and base of the tin with melted butter. Fit the paper around the sides of the tin so that the lip sits flat on the base. Press the circle of paper into the base and brush all the greaseproof paper with more melted butter.

Square tins

Use the same technique as for round tins, but once you've cut the square base and strips, you need to make snips only where the paper fits the corners of the tin.

Loaf tins

Usually, a long strip of paper that covers the base and long sides is enough lining for a loaf tin and this arrangement makes lifting the cake out very easy. If the tin needs lining fully, add 2 further strips of paper at the short ends.

Shallow rectangular and Swiss roll tins

Cut a rectangle of greaseproof paper that is 8 cm (3 inches) longer and wider than the cake tin. Press the paper into the greased tin, snipping it at the corners so that it fits neatly.

Sandwich tins

Draw and cut out circles of greaseproof paper, using the sandwich tins as a guide. Grease the tins and line their bases with the greaseproof paper circles. Alternatively, grease the tins, tip in a little flour and tilt each tin so that the flour coats the base and sides. Tap out the excess flour.

Ring tins

Brush the ring tin thoroughly with melted butter. Tip a little flour into the base of the tin and tilt it until the base and sides are evenly coated with flour. Then tap out the excess flour.

Paper cake liners

These tin liners are like giant paper muffin cases and can be bought to slip into loaf tins and round cake tins. Although they are not readily available in many sizes, they are easy to use and particularly convenient if you need to transport your cakes to fêtes and parties.

Cake-making methods

There are several basic techniques used in cake making. Being aware of the different processes involved will make sure you have good results every time, so if you've not made cakes before, take a look at the following tips.

Creamed cakes

Creaming is the traditional method of making sandwich cakes and buttery sponges. See the Victoria Sandwich Cake recipe (page 32) for step-by-step instructions. The butter must be very soft

(use a microwave if you forget to leave it out of the refrigerator) so that it has a smooth, creamy consistency when it is beaten with the sugar. When it is thoroughly creamed, the butter and sugar mixture should be much paler in colour than the butter alone was, and it should also be very soft. This stage of the process is often described as being 'light and fluffy'.

The beaten eggs are added a little at a time. If the eggs are added too quickly the mixture will curdle, which might affect the texture of the cake. If this happens, add a little of the flour, before finally stirring in the rest of the flour with a metal spoon.

For convenience, many of the creamed cake recipes in this book are made with the all-in-one method, which uses the same ingredients as a creamed mix but mixes them in one go, giving similar results. A little baking powder is added to compensate for the lack of beating.

Whisked cakes

The whisking method is used to make an aerated, fatless sponge. See the Peach and Redcurrant Cream Sponge (page 51) for step-by-step instructions. It's the air that's trapped in the mixture when the eggs and sugar are beaten together that gives a whisked cake volume. A whisked mixture is more delicate than a creamed mixture, so take care throughout the mixing process to keep it aerated and light.

Standing the bowl over a pan of simmering water will help to speed up whisking. Flour is folded in to stabilize the mixture, and it's important to do this as gently as possible so that the foamy consistency is not lost. Plain flour is used in whisked cakes because there's no need for additional raising agents.

A Genoese sponge is made in the same way as a whisked sponge, but with the addition of melted butter. This makes a moister cake, which keeps for longer.

Melted cakes

This quick and easy method is used for cakes such as gingerbread, in which the butter and sugars are melted together in a pan before being mixed in with the dry ingredients. These cakes have a dense but moist texture and rely on baking powder and bicarbonate of soda to make them rise. It's important to bake the cake as soon as the ingredients are mixed together because the raising agents are activated when the wet and dry ingredients are combined. Melted cakes keep well and often improve in flavour and texture if they are wrapped and stored for a couple of days before being eaten. See Fruity Gingerbread (page 64).

Rubbed-in cakes

Used for muffins, crumble cakes and rock buns, this method resembles the one used for homemade pastry. The butter is rubbed into the flour (sometimes with other dry ingredients like oats) with the fingertips or, more conveniently, in a food processor, before the remaining ingredients are added. With the exception of crumble cakes, rubbed-in cakes contain a small proportion of butter and usually stale quickly. They are generally best eaten on the day they are made or, if kept for longer, reheated before serving. For an example of a recipe using the rubbed-in method, see Crumbly Raspberry and Oat Slices (page 98).

Yeasted cakes

Sweet yeasted cakes are made in a similar way to basic breads, but take a long time to prove because of the richness of the dough. To accelerate the process the yeast should first be mixed with a little warm liquid and a dash of sugar, leaving it for 10 minutes or until frothy. This starts the yeast working and is an indication of whether the yeast is fresh – if it doesn't turn frothy, don't bother to continue until you've bought more yeast.

Kneading yeasted cakes by hand on your work surface will take about 10 minutes. Alternatively, you can use a machine – a table-top electric whisk with a dough hook attachment is ideal. This will take 4–5 minutes and allow you to get on with other things. Check the consistency of the dough during kneading. It should feel soft but not so sticky that it clings to your hands or around the sides of the mixer. If necessary, sprinkle with a little more flour.

Yeasted cakes are left to prove (rise) twice, once in the mixing bowl and again when shaped. The first proving can be accelerated slightly in the microwave. Use full power for 15 seconds (but no longer or the dough might start to cook) and leave for 15 minutes. Repeat 2 or 3 times.

Once the dough has risen until it has doubled in size, it must be knocked back to deflate the air. Do this by simply punching the dough with a clenched fist, so that it's ready to shape or roll before the second proving. If you find when rolling the dough that it keeps shrinking back to its original size, cover it with a cloth and leave it for 10 minutes. You will then find it much easier to work with.

To tell whether a yeasted cake is cooked through, tap it gently on the base, if necessary removing it from its tin first. It should sound hollow. If not, return it to the oven for a bit longer. Yeasted cakes taste best when freshly baked and still slightly warm. They also freeze well for another time, in which case warm them through before serving.

Some basic techniques

Here are some of the standard techniques that crop up repeatedly in the cake recipes.

Softening butter

All cakes made using the creamed method require softened butter. This is most easily done in the microwave, because few of us will remember to remove the butter from the refrigerator well in advance of a baking session. Soften it in a few short bursts, checking each time. The butter should be soft enough that you can push into it with your finger.

Melting chocolate

Break the chocolate into pieces and put it in a heatproof bowl. Rest the bowl over a pan of very gently simmering water, making sure that the base of the bowl doesn't come into contact with the water. Once the chocolate starts to melt, turn off the heat and leave the chocolate until it has completely melted, stirring once or twice until no lumps remain. If you want to melt chocolate in the microwave, use a suitable dish and melt the chocolate on

medium power in 1–2-minute spurts, checking it frequently.

If you are melting chocolate with other ingredients – butter, milk or cream, for example – keep a close eye on the mixture because the high fat content will speed up the melting.

Folding in

Flours, flavourings, melted butter or whisked egg whites are usually 'folded' gently into creamed cake and sponge mixes rather than being beaten in. This is because the aim is to keep the mixture light and aerated. Push a large metal spoon down into the mixture and lift it up and over the

ingredients you've added so that you start folding them together. Keep mixing the ingredients together in this way, using a very gentle action and turning the bowl slowly with your other hand until the ingredients are just blended.

When you are adding whisked egg whites to a mixture, fold in about a quarter of the quantity before adding the remainder. The first batch will be useful in lightening the mixture, particularly if it's very firm, which will make it easier for you to fold in the rest of the eggs.

Levelling

Once a cake mixture has been turned into the baking tin, it needs to be levelled. This is so that firm mixtures like fruit cakes and sponges cook evenly and do not emerge from the oven looking lop-sided, and so that whisked sponges are spread to fill the whole tin. Use the back of a large metal spoon to spread the mixture in an even layer. Spread whisked sponges very gently into the corners of square tins so you don't

deflate all the air you've incorporated. Loose sponges, batters and melted mixtures will usually find their own level.

Checking that a cake is cooked

Try not to be impatient when you are waiting for a cake to cook – no matter how strong the desire to eat it might be! Repeatedly opening the oven door, allowing a rush of cold air into the oven, might cause the cake to sink in the middle. You should check that a cake is cooked shortly before it's due to come out of the oven. If it's slightly domed in the centre,

has a baked colour and doesn't 'give' in the centre when lightly touched with a flattened hand it's ready to remove. Fruit cakes and other deep cakes can be further checked by pushing a fine skewer into the centre. The skewer should come out just clean. If there's still raw mixture clinging to the skewer, pop the cake back in the oven for a little longer.

Exceptions to this rules are really moist chocolate cakes and brownies. Brownies in particular should feel very loose under the crust because of the high sugar content, but they will become firmer as they cool.

Cooling cakes on a wire rack

Most sponge cakes should be removed from the tin as soon as you've taken them out of the oven. Loosening the sides of the cake with a knife will help you to release it if you haven't lined the sides of the tin. Remove the cake carefully because the hot sponge will fall apart easily. Rich fruit cakes, however, should be left in the tin until they have cooled completely.

Whipping cream until peaking

To sandwich or cover sponge cakes use double or whipping cream (or half cream and half crème fraîche or mascarpone) and whisk in a bowl with any additional flavours, such as liqueur, flavour extracts or sugar. Use a hand-held electric whisk or a balloon whisk and beat, vigorously at first and then more slowly as it starts to thicken. The aim is to get the cream to form peaks that only just hold their shape, bearing in mind that the cream will continue to thicken as you spread it over the cake.

Storing cakes

A light, buttery sponge cake definitely tastes at its best – even if it is a little difficult to slice – on the day it's made, but it won't spoil if it's stored for several days. Other cakes, such as gingerbread and parkin, might actually improve in flavour and texture if they are stored for a few days before eating, and rich fruit cakes mature in flavour if they are stored for a month or more. If you are storing a cake for any length of time, keep the lining paper in place because this will help prevent the cake from drying out. Store in an airtight container or wrapped in foil, in a cool place. Avoid putting cakes in the refrigerator, unless hot weather means you've no other way of storing a cake decorated with fresh cream or cream cheese frosting. Light sponge cakes and Madeira cakes also freeze well.

Glacé icing
Using lemon or lime juice instead of water in glacé icing gives a welcome tang that helps balance the sweetness of the sugar. Most icing sugars are free flowing, rather than caking together in lumps in the packet. If you open a pack that's a bit lumpy, sift it first.

PREPARATION TIME: 2 minutes

MAKES: enough to thinly cover the top of an 18–20 cm (7–8 inch) cake

75 g (3 oz) icing sugar
2 teaspoons lemon or lime juice

1 Put the icing sugar in a bowl, sifting it first if it's at all lumpy.

2 Add the juice and beat until smooth. Spread over the warm or cooled cake (depending on the recipe).

Buttercream
The best buttercream is very soft and fluffy with a flavour that's not too overpoweringly sweet.

PREPARATION TIME: 3 minutes

MAKES: enough to sandwich and spread over the top of an 18–20 cm (7–8 inch) cake or to cover the top and sides

100 g (3½ oz) unsalted butter, softened
150 g (5 oz) icing sugar

1 Beat the butter in a bowl with a little of the sugar until smooth.

2 Add the remaining sugar and beat until pale and fluffy. Add a few drops of boiling water and beat for a few moments more.

Variation For a coffee-flavoured alternative, dissolve 1 tablespoon instant espresso powder in 2 teaspoons boiling water and beat into the buttercream.

Cream cheese frosting
This is a lovely tangy frosting with plenty of flavour, and it's great for anyone who doesn't like intensely sugary spreads. Taste for sweetness once it's whisked – you can easily beat in another 25 g (1 oz) sugar if it's not sweet enough.

PREPARATION TIME: 3 minutes

MAKES: enough to sandwich and spread over the top of an 18–20 cm (7–8 inch) cake or to cover the top and sides

200 g (7 oz) full-fat cream cheese

1–2 teaspoons lime or lemon juice

75 g (3 oz) icing sugar

1 Beat the cream cheese in a bowl until it is softened and smooth. Beat in 1 teaspoon of the juice.

2 Add the icing sugar and beat until smooth, adding a little more juice if the mixture is very firm.

Variation Use mascarpone cheese instead of cream cheese. Chill in the refrigerator for an hour if it's too soft to spread.

Coconut frosting

This seriously rich icing is perfect for spreading over the angel cake on page 40, but it's also great for adding a lively flavour to a plain Victoria sandwich, in which case you could match the frosting's tropical theme by sandwiching the cake with a tropical fruit jam.

PREPARATION TIME: 5 minutes

COOKING TIME: 2–3 minutes

MAKES: enough to cover the top and sides of an 18–20 cm (7–8 inch) cake

75 ml (3 fl oz) single cream

50 g (2 oz) creamed coconut, chopped

2–3 teaspoons lemon or lime juice

300 g (10 oz) icing sugar

1 Put the cream and creamed coconut in a small saucepan and heat gently until the coconut has melted.

2 Turn into a bowl and whisk in the lemon or lime juice and icing sugar until it is fairly thick and smooth.

Chocolate ganache

A blend of cream and chocolate, ganache is pure indulgence. Used to top chocolate sponges or cupcakes, it's worth making before you start the cake as it can take a while to set.

PREPARATION TIME: 5 minutes, plus chilling

COOKING TIME: 3 minutes

MAKES: enough to cover an 18–20 cm (7–8 inch) cake

300 ml (½ pint) double cream

300 g (10 oz) plain chocolate, chopped

1 Heat the cream in a small saucepan until it is just bubbling around the edges. Remove from the heat and stir in the chocolate. Turn into a bowl and stir frequently until the chocolate has melted.

2 Chill until the mixture holds it shape before spreading.

Variation To make white chocolate ganache, replace the plain chocolate with white chocolate and heat half the quantity of cream until it bubbles around the edges. Stir in the chopped chocolate until it has melted, then turn into a bowl. Chill until cool, then whisk in the remaining cream until the ganache holds its shape.

Everyday cakes *Fresh fruits and vegetables, aromatic herbs and tangy spices create cakes that are bursting with flavour and light enough to eat at almost any time of day. In this chapter you'll find old favourites with a new twist – a zingy Carrot Cake with ginger and orange, a fabulously moist Rosemary and Apple Madeira – as well as more adventurous combinations, such as the delicious Courgette and Lime Cake. Add frosting or cream or serve plain as the mood takes you – the cakes in this chapter are truly versatile.*

Banana yogurt cake with maple syrup
For the best flavour use bananas that are very ripe and speckled with brown or that are just past the point of eating fresh.

PREPARATION TIME: 15 minutes

COOKING TIME: 50–55 minutes

SERVES 8

2 very ripe bananas

100 g (3½ oz) unsalted butter, softened

75 g (3 oz) light muscovado sugar

6 tablespoons maple syrup, plus extra
  to serve

1 egg, beaten

150 g (5 oz) natural yogurt

250 g (8 oz) self-raising flour

1 teaspoon baking powder

1 Grease and line the base and sides of a 15 cm (6 inch) round cake tin. Grease the paper. Mash the bananas.

2 Cream together the butter and sugar until light and fluffy, then beat in the maple syrup. Stir in the egg, banana and yogurt until evenly mixed.

3 Sift the flour and baking powder over the mixture and stir in gently. Turn the mixture into the tin and level the surface. Bake in a preheated oven, 180°C (350°F), Gas Mark 4, for 50–55 minutes or until a skewer inserted into the centre comes out clean.

4 Transfer to a wire rack to cool. Serve drizzled with extra maple syrup.

Blackberry muffin slice
Light in texture and not too sweet, this is a good breakfast or mid-morning cake, served sliced and buttered. It's best eaten freshly made, preferably slightly warm.

PREPARATION TIME: 10 minutes

COOKING TIME: 50–60 minutes

SERVES 6–8

100 g (3½ oz) **unsalted butter, melted**

175 ml (6 fl oz) **milk**

1 **egg**

250 g (8 oz) **plain flour**

2 teaspoons **baking powder**

150 g (5 oz) **caster sugar, plus extra for dusting**

25 g (1 oz) **porridge oats**

100 g (3½ oz) **fresh blackberries**

1 Grease and line the base and sides of a 500 g (1 lb) loaf tin so that the paper comes about 1 cm (½ inch) above the rim of the tin. Grease the paper.

2 Beat together the butter, milk and egg. Sift the flour and baking powder into a bowl and stir in 150 g (5 oz) sugar, the oats and half the blackberries.

3 Stir in the milk mixture until it is only just combined and turn into the tin.

4 Scatter with the remaining blackberries and bake in a preheated oven, 180°C (350°F), Gas Mark 4, for 50–60 minutes or until well risen, golden and firm to the touch.

5 Leave in the tin for 5 minutes, then transfer to a wire rack and sprinkle with a little extra sugar. Serve warm or cold.

Pumpkin cake with vanilla caramel *Make the most of the relatively short pumpkin season with this autumnal cake. For the rest of the year orange-fleshed squash makes a good substitute.*

PREPARATION TIME: 30 minutes

COOKING TIME: about 55 minutes

SERVES 10

250 g (8 oz) pumpkin (skinned and deseeded weight)

175 g (6 oz) unsalted butter, softened

175 g (6 oz) light muscovado sugar

175 g (6 oz) self-raising flour

1 teaspoon baking powder

2 teaspoons ground coriander

3 eggs

75 g (3 oz) ground almonds

Vanilla caramel

100 g (3½ oz) caster sugar

2 tablespoons single cream

2 teaspoons vanilla extract

1 Grease and line the base and sides of a 20 cm (8 inch) round cake tin. Grease the paper. Finely grate the pumpkin and pat dry on kitchen paper.

2 Put the butter, sugar, flour, baking powder, spice, eggs and almonds in a bowl and beat until smooth and creamy.

3 Stir in the pumpkin, turn into the tin and level the surface. Bake in a preheated oven, 160°C (325°F), Gas Mark 3, for about 45 minutes or until a skewer inserted into the centre comes out clean. Transfer to a wire rack to cool.

4 Make the vanilla caramel. Put the sugar and 4 tablespoons water in a small, heavy-based saucepan and heat gently, stirring, until the sugar dissolves. Bring to the boil and boil until the syrup turns to a golden caramel. Remove from the heat and stir in the cream and vanilla extract. Heat gently until smooth. Transfer the cake to a serving plate and spoon over the caramel. Serve with extra caramel, if liked.

Pumpkin cake with vanilla caramel

Grapefruit and star anise sponge *A whole grapefruit, poached with star anise and blended to a purée, gives this sponge a really moist texture and a full, citrusy flavour.*

PREPARATION TIME: 20 minutes, plus cooling
COOKING TIME: 65–80 minutes
SERVES 8–10

1 grapefruit
6 whole star anise
175 g (6 oz) unsalted butter, softened
200 g (7 oz) golden caster sugar
3 eggs
225 g (7½ oz) self-raising flour
1 teaspoon baking powder
finely grated rind of 1 lemon
4 tablespoons demerara sugar

1 Scrub the grapefruit and trim off a thick slice from each end. Cut the fruit into 8 wedges and put them in a saucepan with the star anise and 300 ml (½ pint) water. Bring to the boil, cover with a lid and simmer gently for 20–30 minutes or until the grapefruit peel is tender. Leave to cool in the liquid.

2 Grease and base-line a 20 cm (8 inch) round cake tin. Lift the pieces of star anise from the pan and reserve. Drain the grapefruit wedges, reserving the syrup, and blend the wedges in a food processor or blender to make a smooth paste.

3 Put the butter, sugar, eggs, flour, baking powder and lemon rind in a bowl and beat until smooth and creamy. Stir in the grapefruit paste until evenly combined and turn into the tin. Level the surface.

4 Bake in a preheated oven, 180°C (350°F), Gas Mark 4, for 45–50 minutes until the cake is just firm to the touch. Drizzle with 4 tablespoons of the reserved poaching liquid, sprinkle with the demerara sugar and scatter with the star anise. Transfer to a wire rack to cool.

Plum polenta cake
Polenta and ground almonds are used instead of flour in this incredibly moist cake. During their short season, apricots or greengages make good alternatives to plums.

PREPARATION TIME: 15 minutes

COOKING TIME: 1 hour

SERVES 10

275 g (9 oz) instant polenta

2 teaspoons baking powder

225 g (7½ oz) golden caster sugar, plus 2 tablespoons

100 g (3½ oz) ground almonds

150 g (5 oz) soured cream

100 ml (3½ fl oz) mild olive oil

finely grated rind of 2 lemons, plus 4 tablespoons juice

3 eggs

350 g (11½ oz) red plums

6 tablespoons clear honey

1 Grease a 23 cm (9 inch) round, spring-form tin or loose-based cake tin. Mix together the polenta, the baking powder, the 225 g (7½ oz) sugar and the ground almonds.

2 Beat together the soured cream, oil, lemon rind, 1 tablespoon of the juice and the eggs and add the mixture to the bowl. Stir well until evenly combined and turn into the tin.

3 Stone the plums and cut into quarters. Scatter the pieces over the surface of the cake in an even layer and sprinkle with 2 tablespoons sugar. Bake in a preheated oven, 180°C (350°F), Gas Mark 4, for about 1 hour or until risen and just firm. A skewer inserted into the cake between the plums should come out clean.

4 Mix together the honey and remaining lemon juice and drizzle over the warm cake. Leave to cool in the tin.

Moist ricotta cake
This cake is delicious with a cup of tea or coffee after a light meal. If you think of it in time, soak the raisins overnight so they've plenty of time to plump up.

PREPARATION TIME: 20 minutes, plus soaking

COOKING TIME: 40 minutes

SERVES 9–10

100 g (3½ oz) raisins

3 tablespoons Marsala

175 g (6 oz) unsalted butter, softened

175 g (6 oz) caster sugar

250 g (8 oz) ricotta cheese

1 teaspoon vanilla extract

3 eggs, separated

150 g (5 oz) self-raising flour

1 teaspoon baking powder

icing sugar, for dusting

1 Grease and base-line an 18 cm (7 inch) square cake tin or a 20 cm (8 inch) round tin. Put the raisins and Marsala in a small bowl and leave them to soak for 30 minutes.

2 Cream together the butter and sugar until light and fluffy. Beat in the ricotta, vanilla extract and egg yolks. Stir in the raisins and any unabsorbed Marsala. In a separate, thoroughly clean bowl whisk the egg whites until peaking.

3 Use a large metal spoon to fold a quarter of the egg whites into the mixture to lighten it, then fold in the remainder.

4 Sift the flour and baking powder into the bowl and fold in until combined. Turn the mixture into the tin and level the surface. Bake in a preheated oven, 180°C (350°F), Gas Mark 4, for 40 minutes or until just firm to the touch. Transfer to a wire rack to cool. Serve dusted with plenty of icing sugar.

Courgette and lime cake

Like some other vegetables, such as carrots, courgettes add a subtle flavour and moist texture to a simple sponge. Smother with glacé icing or cream cheese frosting or leave plain.

PREPARATION TIME: 20 minutes

COOKING TIME: 1 hour

SERVES 10

225 g (7½ oz) courgettes

100 g (3½ oz) unsalted butter, softened

100 g (3½ oz) golden caster sugar

finely grated rind of 2 limes

75 g (3 oz) clear honey

3 eggs

225 g (7½ oz) self-raising flour

1 teaspoon baking powder

50 g (2 oz) hazelnuts, toasted and roughly chopped

Glacé Icing (see page 16) or Cream Cheese Frosting (see page 17)

1 Grease and line the base and sides of an 18 cm (7 inch) round cake tin. Grease the paper. Coarsely grate the courgettes and pat between layers of kitchen paper to remove the excess moisture.

2 Put the butter, sugar, lime rind, honey, eggs, flour and baking powder in a bowl and beat until smooth and creamy. Stir in the courgettes and hazelnuts.

3 Turn the mixture into the tin and level the surface. Bake in a preheated oven, 160°C (325°F), Gas Mark 3, for about 1 hour or until risen and golden and a skewer inserted into the centre comes out clean. Transfer to a wire rack to cool.

4 Place on a serving plate and drizzle the top with glacé icing or spread the top and sides with the frosting.

Fresh ginger and pineapple teabread
Fresh root ginger tastes just as spicy and vibrant in sweet dishes as it does in savouries. Use a very fresh piece so it's really aromatic and juicy.

PREPARATION TIME: 20 minutes

COOKING TIME: 1 hour

SERVES 10

65 g (2½ oz) **fresh root ginger**

½ **small pineapple, about 350 g (11½ oz)**

150 g (5 oz) **unsalted butter, softened**

150 g (5 oz) **golden caster sugar**

3 eggs

225 g (7½ oz) **self-raising flour**

1 teaspoon baking powder

65 g (2½ oz) **icing sugar**

1 Line the base and sides of a 1 kg (2 lb) loaf tin. Grease the paper. Peel the ginger and grate it on to a plate to catch the juices. Cut away the skin from the pineapple. Halve the pineapple and cut out the core. Cut 6 very thin slices and roughly chop the remainder.

2 Put the butter, sugar, eggs, flour, baking powder and grated ginger in a bowl, reserving any ginger juices. Beat until smooth and creamy. Stir in the chopped pineapple.

3 Turn the mixture into the tin and level the surface. Bake in a preheated oven, 160°C (325°F), Gas Mark 3, for about 1 hour or until just firm to the touch and a skewer inserted into the centre comes out clean. Transfer to a wire rack to cool.

4 Mix 2 teaspoons of the ginger juice with the icing sugar (make up with water if necessary) to make a thin icing. Arrange the sliced pineapple along the top of the warm cake and drizzle with the icing.

Victoria sandwich cake
Sandwich with jam for a classic Victoria sponge or, for a more decadent filling, spread with jam and 150 ml (¼ pint) whipped double cream.

PREPARATION TIME: 20 minutes

COOKING TIME: 25 minutes

SERVES 8

175 g (6 oz) unsalted butter, softened

175 g (6 oz) caster sugar

3 eggs, beaten

175 g (6 oz) self-raising flour

5 tablespoons strawberry or raspberry jam

icing sugar, Glacé Icing or Buttercream
(see page 16)

1 Grease and base-line 2 x 18 cm (7 inch) round sandwich tins. Put the butter and sugar in a bowl and beat well until the ingredients are very pale in colour, light and fluffy.

2 Gradually beat in the eggs, a little at a time, beating well after each addition. Make sure the mixture is thick and smooth before each addition of egg. If it starts to curdle, beat in a spoonful of the flour.

3 Sift the flour into the bowl. Using a large metal spoon, fold the flour into the mixture. Don't beat it or overmix, or you will knock out all the air. Divide the mixture between the tins and level the surface. Bake in a preheated oven, 180°C (350°F), Gas Mark 4, for about 25 minutes or until risen and just firm to the touch. Loosen the edges of the sponge and turn out on to a wire rack to cool.

4 Sandwich the cakes with the jam and sprinkle generously with icing sugar or spread with glacé icing or buttercream.

Variation For an 'all-in-one-mix' sandwich cake, put all the ingredients together in a bowl, add 1 teaspoon baking powder and beat until smooth and creamy.

Upside-down rhubarb cake
New-season rhubarb – tender, pink and without any hint of bitterness – will give this cake plenty of tangy flavour and contrast perfectly with the buttery sponge.

PREPARATION TIME: 20 minutes

COOKING TIME: 45–50 minutes

SERVES 6–8

400 g (13 oz) young rhubarb

175 g (6 oz) unsalted butter, softened

175 g (6 oz) golden caster sugar

50 g (2 oz) crystallized ginger, finely sliced

2 eggs, beaten

125 g (4 oz) self-raising flour

½ teaspoon baking powder

50 g (2 oz) ground almonds

1 Grease and base-line a shallow, 23 cm (9 inch) round baking tin. Trim the young rhubarb and cut it into 1 cm (½ inch) slices.

2 Melt 50 g (2 oz) of the butter in a frying pan, add 50 g (2 oz) of the sugar and cook gently for 5 minutes until the sugar has dissolved. Stir in the rhubarb and half the ginger and turn into the tin, spreading the mixture in an even layer.

3 Put the remaining butter and sugar in a bowl with the eggs, flour, baking powder, ground almonds and remaining ginger and beat until smooth and creamy.

4 Turn the mixture into the tin and level the surface. Bake in a preheated oven, 180°C (350°F), Gas Mark 4, for 35–40 minutes or until firm to the touch. Leave for 5 minutes, then invert on to a wire rack and lift away the tin. Peel away the lining paper and serve warm or cold.

Cherry Swiss roll
A light-as-air sponge is rolled up around a fruity filling, in this case cherry sauce. If you are short of time, a thick layer of good raspberry or strawberry jam makes an easy alternative.

PREPARATION TIME: 20 minutes

COOKING TIME: 16–20 minutes

SERVES 8

Filling

400 g (13 oz) can pitted black or red cherries

1½ teaspoons cornflour

2 tablespoons golden caster sugar

Sponge

125 g (4 oz) golden caster sugar, plus extra for dusting

3 large eggs

125 g (4 oz) plain flour

1 Grease and line a 33 x 23 cm (13 x 9 inch) Swiss roll tin. Drain the cherries and blend 100 ml (3½ fl oz) of the juice in a small pan with the cornflour and 2 tablespoons sugar. Roughly chop the cherries, add to the pan and cook gently for 3–4 minutes until thickened. Leave to cool.

2 Make the sponge. Put the sugar and eggs in a large heatproof bowl over a pan of hot water and whisk for 6–8 minutes until the whisk leaves a trail when lifted from the bowl. Remove from the heat and whisk for a further 2 minutes.

3 Sift half the flour into the bowl and use a large metal spoon to fold it in gently. (Don't be too heavy handed or you will knock out all the air.) Sift the remaining flour and fold in. Sprinkle 1 tablespoon water over the mixture and fold in. Turn the mixture into the tin and spread gently to the corners. Bake in a preheated oven, 200°C (400°F), Gas Mark 6, for 10–12 minutes until just firm.

4 Sprinkle a sheet of baking parchment with extra sugar. Invert the cake on to the parchment, peel away the lining paper and trim the edges. Spread with the filling and roll up, starting from a short end. Leave to cool, seam side down, on a wire rack.

Warm pear and cinnamon slice

A spicy, sugary crust covering the pears gives this cake its mouthwatering appeal, particularly if it's served warm with a dollop of cream or crème fraîche.

PREPARATION TIME: 20 minutes

COOKING TIME: 25 minutes

SERVES 8

225 g (7½ oz) self-raising flour

1 teaspoon baking powder

125 g (4 oz) unsalted butter

125 g (4 oz) golden caster sugar

1 egg

125 ml (4 fl oz) milk

3 small juicy pears

25 g (1 oz) pecan nuts, roughly chopped

1 teaspoon ground cinnamon

1 Grease and line the base and sides of a shallow, rectangular 27 x 18 cm (11 x 7 inch) baking tin or similar sized roasting tin. Grease the paper. Put the flour and baking powder in a bowl and add 100 g (3½ oz) of the butter, cut into small pieces. Rub in with the fingertips until the mixture resembles fine breadcrumbs. Stir in all but 3 tablespoons of the sugar.

2 Beat together the egg and milk and add to the bowl. Beat well until evenly combined, then turn into the tin, spreading it in an even layer.

3 Quarter, core and slice the pears and arrange the pieces in lines over the sponge. Scatter with the pecan nuts. Melt the remaining butter and brush over the pears.

4 Mix the remaining sugar with the cinnamon and sprinkle over the pears. Bake in a preheated oven, 180°C (350°F), Gas Mark 4, for 25 minutes or until risen and golden. Leave the cake to cool in the tin for about 20 minutes before serving.

Poppyseed and orange bundt cake *If you do not have a traditional bundt tin, use a plain or fluted ring tin for this light and airy cake.*

PREPARATION TIME: 20 minutes

COOKING TIME: 45 minutes

SERVES 10

300 g (10 oz) self-raising flour, plus extra for dusting

150 g (5 oz) unsalted butter, softened

250 g (8 oz) caster sugar

3 eggs, beaten

3 tablespoons poppyseeds

finely grated rind and juice of 1 orange

1 teaspoon baking powder

250 ml (8 fl oz) buttermilk

100 g (3½ oz) whisky-flavoured orange marmalade

Glacé Icing (see page 16)

1 Butter a 1.5 litre (2½ pint) bundt or ring tin and dust with a little flour, tapping out the excess. Cream together the butter and sugar until light and fluffy. Gradually beat in the eggs. Stir in the poppyseeds, orange rind and half the juice.

2 Sift the flour and baking powder into the bowl and add the buttermilk. Use a large metal spoon to fold in the ingredients until just combined. Turn the mixture into the tin and level the surface.

3 Bake in a preheated oven 160°C (325°F), Gas Mark 3, for 45 minutes or until risen and just firm. A skewer inserted into the centre of the sponge should come out clean. Leave to cool.

4 Turn the cake on to a plate. Melt the marmalade with the remaining orange juice and brush over the surface of the cake. Spoon the glacé icing over the top so it trickles down the sides.

Rosemary and apple Madeira

This is moister than the traditional Madeira cake, but just as buttery and delicious. Serve topped with glacé icing or, for the less sweet toothed, leave it as it is.

PREPARATION TIME: 20 minutes, plus cooling

COOKING TIME: 1¼–1½ hours

SERVES 8–10

1 large cooking apple

190 g (6½ oz) unsalted butter, softened

1½ teaspoons finely chopped rosemary

175 g (6 oz) golden caster sugar

3 eggs

finely grated rind of 1 lemon

225 g (7½ oz) self-raising flour

1 teaspoon baking powder

Glacé Icing (see page 16)

1 Peel, core and dice the apple and put the pieces in a small saucepan with 15 g (½ oz) of the butter, the rosemary and 2 teaspoons water. Cover and cook gently for 8–10 minutes until the apple is soft but not pulpy. Leave to cool.

2 Grease and line the base and sides of a 15 cm (6 inch) round cake tin. Grease the paper. Put the remaining butter, sugar, eggs, lemon rind, flour and baking powder in a bowl and beat until smooth and creamy.

3 Stir in the apple until evenly combined and turn the mixture into the tin. Level the surface and bake in a preheated oven, 160°C (325°F), Gas Mark 3, for 1–1¼ hours until firm to the touch and a skewer inserted into the centre comes out clean. Transfer to a wire rack to cool.

4 Spread the glacé icing over the top of the cake so that it runs down the sides.

Carrot cake
This is a light, spongy carrot cake with the subtle addition of ginger and orange. Even when smothered with the tangy cream cheese frosting, it remains fresh and clean tasting.

PREPARATION TIME: 30 minutes

COOKING TIME: 1 hour

SERVES 10–12

225 g (7½ oz) unsalted butter, softened

225 g (7½ oz) light muscovado sugar

4 eggs

grated rind of 1 orange

175 g (6 oz) self-raising flour

1 teaspoon baking powder

75 g (3 oz) ground hazelnuts

65 g (2½ oz) stem ginger, chopped

300 g (10 oz) carrots, finely grated

75 g (3 oz) raisins

Cream Cheese Frosting (see page 17)

toasted hazelnuts, roughly chopped, to decorate

1 Grease and line the base and sides of a 20 cm (8 inch) round cake tin. Put the butter, sugar, eggs, orange rind, flour, baking powder, ground nuts and ginger together in a bowl and beat until smooth and creamy.

2 Stir in the carrots and raisins until evenly combined and turn the mixture into the tin. Level the surface and bake in a preheated oven, 180°C (350°F), Gas Mark 4, for about 1 hour or until just firm and a skewer inserted into the centre comes out clean. Transfer to a wire rack to cool.

3 Use a palette knife to spread the top and sides of the cake with the frosting. Scatter with toasted nuts.

Tip If you can't obtain ground hazelnuts, grind whole ones in a food processor or use ground almonds.

Coconut frosted angel cake
Angel cake is as good a way to use up leftover egg whites as a pavlova or meringue. This creamy white, airy sponge is smothered in a contrastingly rich coconut frosting.

PREPARATION TIME: 25 minutes

COOKING TIME: 25 minutes

SERVES 10–12

vegetable oil for brushing

150 g (5 oz) plain flour, plus extra for dusting

8 egg whites

1 teaspoon cream of tartar

225 g (7½ oz) caster sugar

2 teaspoons vanilla extract

Coconut Frosting (see page 18)

toasted coconut shavings, to decorate

1 Brush a 1.5 litre (2½ pint) ring tin with oil and coat with flour, tapping out the excess. Beat the egg whites in a large, thoroughly clean bowl until frothy. Add the cream of tartar and beat until peaking.

2 Gradually beat in the sugar, a tablespoonful at a time, beating well after each addition until the mixture is stiff and glossy. Beat in the vanilla extract with the last of the sugar.

3 Sift the flour into the bowl and gently fold it into the mixture, using a large metal spoon. Turn the mixture into the tin and level the surface. Bake in a preheated oven, 160°C (325°F), Gas Mark 3, for about 25 minutes or until firm to the touch and a skewer inserted into the centre comes out clean.

4 Invert the cake on to a wire rack but don't remove the tin. When cool, loosen the edges of the tin and turn the cake out on to a flat plate. Spread with coconut frosting and scatter with the toasted coconut shavings.

Rye, raisin and aniseed teabread

A grainy, not too sweet teabread with the flavour of ground aniseed. It's great for snacks, sliced and buttered, and even goes well with a sharp, salty cheese.

PREPARATION TIME: 10 minutes, plus soaking

COOKING TIME: 40 minutes

SERVES 8

100 g (3½ oz) raisins

200 ml (7 fl oz) ale or stout

100 g (3½ oz) molasses sugar

1 teaspoon aniseeds

1 egg, beaten

150 g (5 oz) rye flour

100 g (3½ oz) wholemeal self-raising flour

½ teaspoon baking powder

1 Put the raisins in a large bowl with the ale or stout and leave to soak for 1 hour. Grease and line the base and sides of a 500 g (1 lb) loaf tin. Grease the paper.

2 Stir the sugar into the raisin mixture. Use a pestle and mortar to crush the aniseeds and add them to the bowl with the egg, flours and baking powder. Mix well and turn into the tin.

3 Level the surface and bake in a preheated oven, 180°C (350°F), Gas Mark 4, for about 40 minutes until firm and a skewer inserted into the centre comes out clean. Transfer to a wire rack to cool.

Tip If you can't get hold of aniseeds, use fennel seeds instead.

Italian pine nut cake

This cake is not very sweet, but it does have a delicate nuttiness and amazingly fluffy texture. It's great with a cup of coffee or as an accompaniment to poached or grilled fruit.

PREPARATION TIME: 25 minutes

COOKING TIME: 50–60 minutes

SERVES 12

4 eggs, separated

275 g (9 oz) caster sugar

finely grated rind of 1 orange

225 ml (7½ fl oz) mild olive oil

100 ml (3½ fl oz) Marsala or dessert wine

100 ml (3½ fl oz) orange juice

350 g (11½ oz) self-raising flour

100 g (3½ oz) pine nuts, toasted

icing sugar, for dusting

1 Grease and base-line a 23 cm (9 inch) round, spring-form tin or loose-based cake tin. Put the egg yolks, sugar and orange rind in a bowl and beat until thickened and pale.

2 Whisk in the olive oil, then the Marsala or wine and orange juice. Sift the flour into the bowl and gently stir in.

3 Whisk the egg whites in a thoroughly clean bowl until peaking. Gently fold into the mixture along with 75 g (3 oz) of the pine nuts.

4 Tip the mixture into the tin, spreading it gently to the edges. Scatter with the reserved pine nuts and bake in a preheated oven, 180°C (350°F), Gas Mark 4, for 50–60 minutes or until just firm and a skewer inserted into the centre comes out clean. Transfer to a wire rack and lightly dust with icing sugar.

Sticky toffee cake

Not many cake lovers will resist the temptation to come back for more of this gorgeous treat. Like the pudding that it copies, it's wickedly good served with cream!

PREPARATION TIME: 20 minutes, plus cooling

COOKING TIME: about 1¼ hours

SERVES 10

125 g (4 oz) dates, stoned and chopped

125 g (4 oz) unsalted butter, softened

100 g (3½ oz) caster sugar

2 teaspoons vanilla extract

3 eggs

175 g (6 oz) self-raising flour

1 teaspoon baking powder

Topping

150 ml (¼ pint) double cream

175 g (6 oz) light muscovado sugar

75 g (3 oz) unsalted butter

1 Grease and line the base and sides of an 18 cm (7 inch) round, spring-form tin or loose-based cake tin. Grease the paper. Put the dates in a small pan with 150 ml (¼ pint) water and bring to the boil. Reduce the heat and cook gently for 5 minutes or until the dates are soft and pulpy. Turn into a bowl to cool.

2 Make the topping. Put the cream, sugar and butter in a small saucepan and heat gently until the sugar dissolves. Bring to the boil and let the mixture bubble for 6–8 minutes until thickened. Cool.

3 Put the butter, sugar, vanilla extract, eggs, flour and baking powder in a bowl and beat until smooth and creamy. Stir in the date purée and 100 g (3½ oz) of the topping. Turn the mixture into the tin and level the surface. Bake in a preheated oven, 180°C (350°F), Gas Mark 4, for about 40 minutes or until just firm.

4 Tip the remaining topping over the cake and return to the oven for 20 minutes. Transfer to a wire rack, leaving the lining paper attached until the cake has cooled.

Sticky toffee cake

Lemon drizzle cake

Ask anyone to list their favourite cakes, and this will almost certainly be one of them. Intensely lemony and with an irresistibly sugary crust, this version is one of the best.

PREPARATION TIME: 20 minutes

COOKING TIME: 50–60 minutes

SERVES 8–10

225 g (7½ oz) unsalted butter, softened

225 g (7½ oz) caster sugar

finely grated rind of 3 lemons, plus 100 ml (3½ fl oz) lemon juice

4 eggs, beaten

250 g (8 oz) self-raising flour

1 teaspoon baking powder

75 g (3 oz) ground almonds

100 g (3½ oz) granulated sugar

1 Grease and line the base and sides of a 20 cm (8 inch) round cake tin or an 18 cm (7 inch) square tin. Grease the paper. Cream together the butter, caster sugar and the lemon rind until light and fluffy.

2 Beat in the eggs, a little at a time, beating well between each addition. Add a little of the flour if the mixture starts to curdle. Sift the flour and baking powder into the bowl, add the ground almonds and 2 tablespoons of the lemon juice and gently fold in using a large metal spoon.

3 Turn the mixture into the tin and level the surface. Bake in a preheated oven, 180°C (350°F), Gas Mark 4, for about 45 minutes or until just firm and a skewer inserted into the centre comes out clean.

4 Meanwhile, mix together the remaining lemon juice with the granulated sugar. Transfer the cake to a wire rack. Give the lemon mixture a good stir and spoon it over the cake. As the cake cools the syrup will sink into the cake, leaving a sugary crust.

Apple and cranberry streusel

There's only a tenuous link between this cake and a traditional German streusel, but it is easy to make and is delicious served slightly warm with a dollop of cream.

PREPARATION TIME: 20 minutes

COOKING TIME: 50–60 minutes

SERVES 6–8

250 g (8 oz) self-raising flour

175 g (6 oz) unsalted butter, diced

175 g (6 oz) golden caster sugar, plus
  2 tablespoons

1 egg

4 tart dessert apples, such as Granny Smith

50 g (2 oz) dried cranberries

icing sugar, for dusting

1 Grease an 18 cm (7 inch) round spring-form tin or loose-based cake tin. Put the flour in a food processor and add the butter, cut into small pieces. Blend until the mixture resembles fine breadcrumbs. Add 175 g (6 oz) sugar and blend until the mixture just starts to make a coarse crumble.

2 Spoon out 175 g (6 oz) of the mixture and add the egg to the remainder in the blender. Blend to a firm paste. Turn the paste into the base of the tin, pressing it down gently in an even layer.

3 Peel, core and slice the apples. Toss in a bowl with the cranberries and the remaining caster sugar. Scatter the fruit into the tin and sprinkle with the reserved crumble mix.

4 Bake in a preheated oven, 180°C (350°F), Gas Mark 4, for 50–60 minutes or until deep golden. Leave to cool in the tin and serve lightly dusted with icing sugar.

Spicy beetroot cake

This cake might be an acquired taste, but it's certainly one for beetroot lovers. Crushed juniper adds depth to the flavour, but a spoonful of mixed spice or ginger would be good too.

PREPARATION TIME: 20 minutes

COOKING TIME: 25 minutes

SERVES 8

12 juniper berries

50 g (2 oz) pecan nuts, plus extra, roughly chopped, to decorate

175 g (6 oz) unsalted butter, softened

175 g (6 oz) light muscovado sugar

3 eggs

150 g (5 oz) self-raising flour

1 teaspoon baking powder

200 g (7 oz) raw beetroot, grated

Cream Cheese Frosting (see page 17)

1 Grease and base-line 2 x 18 cm (7 inch) sandwich tins. Use a pestle and mortar to crush the juniper berries and tip them into a food processor with the pecan nuts. Blend until ground.

2 Put the butter, sugar, eggs, flour and baking powder into a bowl. Add the ground nuts and spice and beat until the mixture is smooth and creamy. Whisk or stir in the grated beetroot.

3 Divide the mixture between the tins and level the surface. Bake in a preheated oven, 180°C (350°F), Gas Mark 4, for about 25 minutes or until just firm to the touch. Transfer to a wire rack to cool.

4 Sandwich the cakes with half the cream cheese frosting and spread the remainder over the top. Decorate with the roughly chopped pecans.

Spicy beetroot cake

Thyme and kumquat cake

Thyme is one of the most versatile of all herbs, and lemon thyme is particularly good in sweet dishes. This cake is lovely when you want something a bit different.

PREPARATION TIME: 20 minutes, plus cooling

COOKING TIME: about 1 hour

SERVES 8–10

150 g (5 oz) kumquats

190 g (6½ oz) golden caster sugar

175 g (6 oz) unsalted butter, softened

3 eggs

125 g (4 oz) self-raising flour

100 g (3½ oz) self-raising wholemeal flour

1 teaspoon baking powder

2 teaspoons chopped thyme

75 g (3 oz) icing sugar

thyme sprigs, to decorate

1 Put the kumquats in a small saucepan with 15 g (½ oz) of the sugar and 100 ml (3½ fl oz) water. Heat gently until the sugar dissolves, then cover and cook over a gentle heat for 5 minutes. Drain, reserving the liquid, and leave to cool. Grease a 1 kg (2 lb) loaf tin and line the base and long sides with a strip of greaseproof paper. Grease the paper.

2 Thinly slice the kumquats. Put the remaining sugar, butter, eggs, flours, baking powder and thyme in a bowl and beat until smooth and creamy. Stir in the kumquat slices and 2 tablespoons of the juice.

3 Turn the mixture into the tin and level the surface. Bake in a preheated oven, 160°C (325°F), Gas Mark 3, for 50–55 minutes or until just firm and a skewer inserted into the centre comes out clean. Transfer to a wire rack to cool.

4 Mix together the icing sugar and 1 tablespoon of the remaining syrup. Drizzle over the cake and serve scattered with thyme sprigs.

Peach and redcurrant cream sponge *Whisked*

sponges have an incredibly light and airy texture but keep for only a day, unless you make a Genoese sponge (see below).

PREPARATION TIME: 20 minutes

COOKING TIME: 20–25 minutes

SERVES 8–10

100 g (3½ oz) caster sugar

4 eggs

100 g (3½ oz) plain flour

Filling

100 g (3½ oz) redcurrants

150 ml (¼ pint) double or whipping cream

1 tablespoon caster sugar, plus extra for dusting

1 ripe, juicy peach, sliced

1 Grease and base-line 2 x 20 cm (8 inch) sandwich tins. Put the sugar and eggs in a large heatproof bowl over a pan of hot water and whisk for 6–8 minutes or until the whisk leaves a trail when lifted from the bowl. Remove from the heat and whisk for a further 2 minutes.

2 Sift half the flour into the bowl and fold in using a large metal spoon. Sift and fold in the remaining flour.

3 Turn the mixture into the tins and spread gently to the edges. Bake in a preheated oven, 190°C (375°F), Gas Mark 5, for 20–25 minutes or until just firm to the touch. Transfer to a wire rack to cool.

4 Reserve a few redcurrant sprigs. Remove the berries of the remainder by running the stalks between the tines of a fork. Whip the cream with 1 tablespoon sugar and spread it over one cake layer. Scatter with the fruits and place the second cake on top. Decorate with the reserved sprigs and dust with a little more sugar.

Variation A Genoese sponge keeps longer because of the addition of butter. To make a Genoese sponge melt 50 g (2 oz) unsalted butter and leave to cool. Pour half the cooled butter around the edges of the whisked mixture after sifting in the first batch of flour. Fold in with the flour. Add the remaining melted butter with the second batch of flour.

Rich and fruity *This chapter certainly provides a choice of fruit cakes that are truly fit for a feast. The Chunky Fruit and Nut Cake is the classic cake to cover with marzipan and icing, while doing the same to a Jamaican Rum Cake produces a celebration cake with a spicy undertone and vibrant kick.*

Don't forget that fruit and nuts can also be combined to make healthier alternatives. Cakes such as the Apple and Prune Cake or Malty Fruit Cake are packed full of goodness, and a slice makes a nourishing, wholesome snack. Many fruit cakes keep very well, making them ideal for unexpected guests.

Spicy date parkin

This sticky, treacly parkin will appeal to those who'd rather not wander too far from the path of healthy eating! It tastes just as good several days after baking.

PREPARATION TIME: 15 minutes, plus soaking

COOKING TIME: 55 minutes

SERVES 12

250 g (8 oz) dried dates, roughly chopped

250 ml (8 fl oz) fresh apple juice

175 g (6 oz) black treacle

175 g (6 oz) golden syrup

100 g (3½ oz) unsalted butter

125 g (4 oz) plain flour

125 g (4 oz) self-raising wholemeal flour

1 teaspoon bicarbonate of soda

1 tablespoon ground mixed spice

225 g (7½ oz) fine or medium oatmeal

1 Put the dates and apple juice in a small saucepan and bring to the boil. Remove from the heat and leave to stand for 30 minutes. Grease and line the base and sides of a 20 cm (8 inch) square cake tin. Grease the paper.

2 Put the treacle, syrup and butter in a medium-sized saucepan and heat gently until the butter has melted. Mix together the flours, bicarbonate of soda, spice and oatmeal in a large bowl.

3 Pour the melted ingredients into the bowl with the dates and apple juice and stir until all the ingredients are well mixed. Turn the mixture into the tin and level the surface.

4 Bake in a preheated oven, 160°C (325°F), Gas Mark 3, for about 50 minutes or until a skewer inserted into the centre comes out clean. Leave to cool in the tin. (Don't worry if the cake sinks slightly in the centre as it cools – it will be particularly moist and gooey.)

Variation You can use other dried fruits, such as apricots, prunes or figs, instead of the dates.

Red fruit teabread
Grinding your own almonds in a blender or food processor will always give the freshest, nuttiest flavour. This fruity slice can be served plain or lightly buttered.

PREPARATION TIME: 10 minutes, plus soaking

COOKING TIME: about 45 minutes

SERVES 8

200 g (7 oz) mixture of dried red fruits, such as sour cherries, cranberries and strawberries

150 ml (¼ pint) hot fruit tea, such as raspberry, strawberry or cranberry

100 g (3½ oz) blanched almonds

100 g (3½ oz) light muscovado sugar

1 egg, beaten

75 g (3 oz) self-raising flour

½ teaspoon baking powder

demerara sugar, to serve

1 Put the dried fruits in a bowl, add the fruit tea and leave to stand for 1 hour until most of the tea has been absorbed.

2 Grease and line the base and long sides of a 500 g (1 lb) loaf tin. Grease the paper. Roughly chop half the almonds, then grind the remainder in a food processor or blender.

3 Stir the chopped and ground almonds, sugar, egg, flour and baking powder into the soaked fruit and stir until combined.

4 Turn the mixture into the tin and level the surface. Bake in a preheated oven, 180°C (350°F), Gas Mark 4, for about 45 minutes or until firm to the touch and a skewer inserted into the centre comes out clean. Transfer to a wire rack to cool and sprinkle with demerara sugar.

Jamaican rum cake
The rum in this moist, fruity cake has a vibrant kick. Dark and spicy, it's a good cake for winter and can be served plain or covered with marzipan and icing as a Christmas cake.

PREPARATION TIME: 25 minutes, plus soaking

COOKING TIME: 2½–3 hours

SERVES 12–16

625 g (1¼ lb) mixed dried fruit

100 g (3½ oz) glacé cherries, halved

250 ml (8 fl oz) dark rum

2 tablespoons black treacle

175 g (6 oz) unsalted butter, softened

175 g (6 oz) dark muscovado sugar

4 eggs, beaten

200 g (7 oz) self-raising flour

2 tablespoons ground ginger

1 Put the fruit and cherries in a large bowl and pour in the rum. Give the mixture a good stir, cover and leave for 24 hours, stirring occasionally.

2 Grease and line the base and sides of a 19–20 cm (7½–8 inch) round cake tin or a 16–18 cm (6½–7 inch) square tin. Grease the paper. Drain 400 g (13 oz) of the fruit from the bowl using a slotted spoon and blend in a food processor with the treacle.

3 Beat together the butter and sugar until creamy. Gradually beat in the eggs, a little at a time, adding a little of the flour if the mixture starts to curdle.

4 Stir in the remaining flour and ginger, whole fruits and any unabsorbed rum, and the fruit purée. Stir with a large metal spoon until well mixed.

5 Turn the mixture into the tin and level the surface. Bake in a preheated oven, 150°C (300°F), Gas Mark 2, for 2½–3 hours or until firm and a skewer inserted into the centre comes out clean. Leave to cool in the tin.

Apple and prune cake

This is a healthy, wholesome cake that's good for a late breakfast or as a lunchbox filler. Other dried fruits, such as figs, apricots or dates, can be used instead of prunes.

PREPARATION TIME: 15 minutes

COOKING TIME: 40 minutes

SERVES 8

150 g (5 oz) self-raising flour

1 teaspoon baking powder

125 g (4 oz) fine or medium oatmeal

100 g (3½ oz) fruit or nut muesli, plus
   4 tablespoons

2 teaspoons ground mixed spice

25 g (1 oz) sunflower seeds

175 g (6 oz) demerara sugar, plus
   1 tablespoon

1 large cooking apple, such as Bramley

175 g (6 oz) no-soak pitted prunes, halved

2 eggs

125 g (4 oz) unsalted butter, melted

4 tablespoons apple juice

1 Grease and line the base and sides of an 18 cm (7 inch) square cake tin or a 20 cm (8 inch) round, loose-based tin or a spring-form tin. Grease the paper.

2 Mix together the flour, baking powder, oatmeal, 100 g (3½ oz) muesli, spice, seeds and 175 g (6 oz) sugar.

3 Peel, core and roughly chop the apple and add to the bowl with the prunes. Beat the eggs with the butter and apple juice and stir in until evenly combined.

4 Turn the mixture into the tin and level the surface. Sprinkle with the remaining muesli and sugar and bake in a preheated oven, 180°C (350°F), Gas Mark 4, for 40 minutes or until just firm to the touch. Transfer to a wire rack to cool.

Malty fruit cake

This is a quick, easy and wholesome cake, perfect for when you want to make something quickly for tea or snacks. It's moist and fruity as it is, or you can serve it lightly buttered.

PREPARATION TIME: 10 minutes, plus soaking

COOKING TIME: 50 minutes

SERVES 8

175 g (6 oz) luxury mixed dried fruit

125 g (4 oz) dark muscovado sugar

3 tablespoons malt extract

100 g (3½ oz) shredded bran or bran-flake cereal

1 teaspoon ground cinnamon

½ teaspoon freshly grated nutmeg

300 ml (½ pint) milk

150 g (5 oz) self-raising flour

1 Grease and line the base and sides of a 500 g (1 lb) loaf tin, making the paper come at least 1 cm (½ inch) above the rim of the tin. Grease the paper. Mix together the fruit, sugar, malt extract, bran, spices and milk in a bowl and leave to stand for 20 minutes.

2 Stir in the flour and turn the mixture into the tin. Bake in a preheated oven, 160°C (325°F), Gas Mark 3, for about 50 minutes or until a skewer inserted into the centre comes out clean. Transfer to a wire rack to cool.

Moist cherry and almond cake

This cake is so fabulously moist and almondy that it's difficult to resist. It combines creaming and whisking techniques, which gives it a light, airy texture.

PREPARATION TIME: 25 minutes

COOKING TIME: 1–1¼ hours

SERVES 12

200 g (7 oz) natural glacé cherries

150 g (5 oz) self-raising flour

250 g (8 oz) unsalted butter, softened

250 g (8 oz) golden caster sugar

5 eggs, separated

1 teaspoon almond extract

1 tablespoon lemon juice

150 g (5 oz) ground almonds

15 g (½ oz) flaked almonds

1 Grease and line a 1.25 kg (2½ lb) loaf tin. Grease the paper. Rinse and dry the cherries, cut them in half and toss in 1 tablespoon of the flour.

2 Cream together the butter and 200 g (7 oz) of the sugar until the mixture is light and fluffy. Beat in the egg yolks, almond extract and lemon juice. Sift the remaining flour into the bowl and stir in with a large metal spoon.

3 Whisk the egg whites in a thoroughly clean bowl until peaking. Gradually whisk in the remaining sugar, then fold in the ground almonds.

4 Fold a quarter of the whisked mixture into the creamed mixture to lighten it, then fold in the remainder, along with half the cherries. Turn the mixture into the tin and level the surface. Scatter the cake with the remaining cherries and flaked almonds.

5 Bake in a preheated oven, 180°C (350°F), Gas Mark 4, for about 1–1¼ hours or until golden and a skewer inserted into the centre comes out clean. Leave to cool in the tin.

Sultana flapjack cake

This recipe contains all the lovely flavours and textures of flapjacks. When taken from the oven, it should be only just firm to the touch. Overcooking will quickly dry it out.

PREPARATION TIME: 15 minutes, plus soaking

COOKING TIME: about 1 hour

SERVES 10

200 g (7 oz) sultanas

150 ml (¼ pint) apple juice

125 g (4 oz) porridge oats

100 g (3½ oz) light muscovado sugar

100 g (3½ oz) golden syrup, plus extra to glaze

175 g (6 oz) unsalted butter

1 tablespoon ground ginger

2 eggs

125 g (4 oz) self-raising flour

½ teaspoon baking powder

1 Grease and line the base and sides of an 18 cm (7 inch) round cake tin. Grease the paper. Put the sultanas and apple juice in a small saucepan and bring to the boil. Remove from the heat and stand for 30 minutes.

2 Put the oats in a frying pan and heat gently, stirring, for 5 minutes or until they just start to toast. Remove from the heat and add the sugar, syrup, butter and ginger. Stir frequently until the butter melts.

3 Drain 125 g (4 oz) of the oat mixture and reserve. Tip the remainder into a bowl and add the eggs, flour and baking powder. Beat well until the mixture is combined, then stir in the sultanas and any unabsorbed juice.

4 Turn the mixture into the tin and level the surface. Spoon the reserved oat mixture over the top. Bake in a preheated oven, 180°C (350°F), Gas Mark 4, for about 1 hour until risen and just firm to the touch. Drizzle with a little extra syrup and leave in the tin to cool.

Sweet saffron cake
This cake is made using a yeasted dough and is somewhere between a cake and a bread in texture and flavour. It is at its best served very fresh, sliced and buttered.

PREPARATION TIME: 25 minutes, plus proving

COOKING TIME: 45 minutes

SERVES 8–10

1 teaspoon saffron threads

225 ml (7½ fl oz) hand-hot milk

2 teaspoons easy-blend dried yeast

100 g (3½ oz) caster sugar, plus 1 teaspoon

500 g (1 lb) strong bread flour

1 egg, beaten

200 g (7 oz) salted butter, very soft

250 g (8 oz) luxury mixed dried fruit

1 Crumble the saffron threads into the milk and stir in the yeast and 1 teaspoon sugar. Leave to stand for 10 minutes or until frothy.

2 Put the flour and remaining sugar in a large bowl. Make a well in the centre and add the egg. Slice in the butter and add the yeasted milk. Use a round-bladed knife to mix the ingredients to a soft dough, adding a little extra flour if the dough feels sticky.

3 Turn out on to a floured surface and knead gently for 10 minutes or until smooth and elastic. Transfer to a lightly oiled bowl, cover with clingfilm and leave to rise in a warm place for 1–2 hours or until it has doubled in size.

4 Grease an 18 cm (7 inch) round cake tin. Knock back the dough (see page 12) and knead in the fruit. Shape into a large round. Drop it into the tin, cover loosely with oiled clingfilm and leave to rise for about 1 hour or until doubled in size.

5 Bake in a preheated oven, 190°C (375°F), Gas Mark 5, for 40 minutes or until deep golden. Remove from the tin and return to the oven for 5 minutes. Transfer to a wire rack to cool.

Fruity gingerbread

This tray bake is perfect for feeding a crowd and keeps well for several days. It's mildly gingery, rather than spicily hot, so add more ground or stem ginger if you wish.

PREPARATION TIME: 15 minutes

COOKING TIME: 1 hour

SERVES 12–16

450 g (14½ oz) plain flour

2 teaspoons ground ginger

2 teaspoons baking powder

1 teaspoon bicarbonate of soda

175 g (6 oz) lightly salted butter

225 g (7½ oz) molasses sugar

325 g (11 oz) black treacle

300 ml (½ pint) milk

1 egg, beaten

65 g (2½ oz) stem ginger, finely chopped

250 g (8 oz) mixed dried fruit

double quantity Glacé Icing (see page 16)

1 Grease and line the base and long sides of a 28 x 23 cm (11 x 9 inch) roasting tin or a similar sized baking tin with a strip of greaseproof paper so it's easy to lift out after baking. Line the ends of the tin and grease the paper. Put the flour, ginger, baking powder and bicarbonate of soda in a bowl.

2 Melt the butter in a small saucepan with the sugar and treacle. Remove from the heat and stir in the milk, then the egg.

3 Stir the mixture into the dry ingredients with the stem ginger and dried fruit and pour into the tin. Level the surface and bake in a preheated oven, 160°C (325°F), Gas Mark 3, for 50–55 minutes or until it is firm to the touch and a skewer inserted into the centre comes out clean. Leave to cool for 10 minutes. Don't worry if it sinks a bit in the middle; gingerbread often does.

4 Lift the cake from the tin, drizzle with the glacé icing and leave to cool.

Fruity gingerbread

Stollen

A rich, sweet dough with the merest hint of alcohol is perfect for tucking into over the festive season. Pistachio nuts add a vibrant colour, but almonds are an equally good alternative.

PREPARATION TIME: 25 minutes, plus soaking and proving

COOKING TIME: 30 minutes

SERVES 12

100 g (3½ oz) sultanas

50 g (2 oz) candied peel, chopped

4 tablespoons dark rum

2 teaspoons easy-blend dried yeast

50 g (2 oz) caster sugar, plus 1 teaspoon

200 ml (7 fl oz) hand-hot milk

350 g (11½ oz) strong bread flour

finely grated rind of 1 lemon

75 g (3 oz) pistachio nuts

50 g (2 oz) butter, melted

250 g (8 oz) white marzipan

icing sugar, for dusting

1 Put the sultanas, peel and rum in a bowl and leave to soak for 1 hour. Stir the yeast and 1 teaspoon sugar into the milk in a bowl and leave for 10 minutes or until frothy.

2 Mix together the flour, lemon rind, remaining sugar and nuts in a large bowl. Add the butter and yeasted milk and mix to a soft dough with a round-bladed knife, adding a little more flour if the dough feels sticky.

3 Turn out on to a floured surface and knead for 10 minutes or until smooth and elastic. Transfer to a lightly oiled bowl, cover with clingfilm and leave to rise in a warm place for 1–2 hours or until doubled in size. Shape the marzipan into a sausage about 25 cm (10 inches) in length.

4 Knock back the dough (see page 12) and knead in the fruit. Roll it out to an oval about 30 x 18 cm (12 x 7 inches) and lay the marzipan slightly to one side of the centre. Brush the long edges of the dough with water and fold the wider piece of dough over the filling, pressing down gently.

5 Transfer the dough to a greased baking sheet, cover with oiled clingfilm and leave to rise for about 45 minutes or until doubled in size. Bake in a preheated oven, 190°C (375°F), Gas Mark 5, for 30 minutes or until golden. Transfer to a wire rack to cool. Serve generously dusted with icing sugar.

Florentine fruit cake

This cake is moist and semi-rich. It's topped with a delicious, sugary crust of fruit and nuts that looks really stunning, especially when it's glistening with drizzled honey.

PREPARATION TIME: 30 minutes

COOKING TIME: 1¾ hours

SERVES 12

250 g (8 oz) **unsalted butter, softened**

250 g (8 oz) **golden caster sugar**

4 **eggs, beaten**

2 **teaspoons vanilla extract**

275 g (9 oz) **plain flour, plus 2 tablespoons**

1 **tablespoon ground mixed spice**

125 g (4 oz) **flaked almonds**

125 g (4 oz) **glacé cherries, halved**

150 g (5 oz) **sultanas**

150 g (5 oz) **raisins**

1 **tablespoon double cream**

50 g (2 oz) **whole sweet almonds**

honey, to serve

1 Grease and line the base and sides of an 18 cm (7 inch) round cake tin or a 15 cm (6 inch) square tin. Grease the paper. Cream 225 g (7½ oz) of the butter with 225 g (7½ oz) sugar until light and fluffy.

2 Gradually beat in the eggs, a little at a time, beating well after each addition. Stir in the vanilla extract.

3 Sift 275 g (9 oz) flour and the spice into the bowl. Using a large metal spoon, fold the flour into the mixture. Add 75 g (3 oz) each of the flaked almonds and cherries and 125 g (4 oz) each of the sultanas and raisins. Mix until just combined. Turn the mixture into the tin and level the surface.

4 Melt the remaining butter in a small pan and stir in the remaining sugar. Add 2 tablespoons of flour, the cream and the remaining fruit and nuts, including the whole almonds. Scatter over the cake mixture and bake in a preheated oven, 150°C (300°F), Gas Mark 2, for 1¾ hours or until a skewer inserted into the centre comes out clean. Leave to cool in the tin. Serve drizzled with honey.

Simnel cake

A classic Easter simnel cake has a delicious layer of marzipan running through the centre, which mingles in with the flavours of the fruit cake.

PREPARATION TIME: 30 minutes

COOKING TIME: 2–2½ hours

SERVES 16–18

175 g (6 oz) unsalted butter, softened

175 g (6 oz) golden caster sugar

75 g (3 oz) fresh root ginger, grated

3 eggs

225 g (7½ oz) plain flour

2 teaspoons ground mixed spice

500 g (1 lb) mixed dried fruit

500 g (1 lb) white marzipan

icing sugar, for dusting

1 egg white, lightly beaten

physalis, to decorate

1 Grease and line the base and sides of an 18 cm (7 inch) round cake tin. Grease the paper. Cream together the butter, sugar and ginger until light and fluffy. Gradually beat in the eggs, adding a little of the flour if it starts to curdle. Stir in the flour and spice, then the dried fruit.

2 Spoon half the mixture into the tin and spread in an even layer. Roll out half the marzipan on a surface dusted with icing sugar to a round slightly smaller than the tin. Lay the paste over the cake mixture and cover with the remaining cake mix.

3 Bake in a preheated oven, 150°C (300°F), Gas Mark 2, for 2–2½ hours or until a skewer inserted into the centre comes out clean. Cool in the tin.

4 To decorate, brush the top with a little egg white. Roll out the remaining almond paste to an 18 cm (7 inch) round and lay over the cake. Crimp the edges and brush with beaten egg white. Cook under the grill, watching closely, for 2 minutes or until the paste is golden. Cool, then decorate with sugar-dusted physalis.

Chunky fruit and nut cake

Because the ingredients for this cake are melted together in a saucepan, no creaming is involved, and the fruit plumps up in the sweet, buttery juices.

PREPARATION TIME: 20 minutes, plus cooling
COOKING TIME: 3 hours–3 hours 10 minutes
SERVES 24

275 g (9 oz) unsalted butter
325 g (11 oz) light muscovado sugar
1.25 kg (2½ lb) mixed dried fruit
finely grated rind and juice of 1 lemon
200 ml (7 fl oz) sherry
4 tablespoons brandy
2 tablespoons ground mixed spice
100 g (3½ oz) Brazil nuts, roughly chopped
100 g (3½ oz) hazelnuts, roughly chopped
100 g (3½ oz) ground hazelnuts
5 eggs, beaten
375 g (12 oz) plain flour

1 Slice the butter into a large, heavy-based saucepan and add the sugar, dried fruit, lemon rind and juice, sherry, brandy and mixed spice. Heat gently until the butter has melted, stirring frequently. Simmer gently for about 10 minutes or until the juices are thick and syrupy. Leave to cool for at least 30 minutes.

2 Grease and line the base and sides of a 23 cm (9 inch) round cake tin or a 20 cm (8 inch) square tin. Grease the paper. Stir all the nuts and the eggs into the fruit mixture.

3 Add the flour and mix until evenly combined. Turn the mixture into the tin and level the surface. Bake in a preheated oven, 140°C (275°F), Gas Mark 1, for 2¾–3 hours or until a skewer inserted into the centre comes out clean.

4 Leave to cool in the tin, then remove and wrap in foil until needed.

Tip This is a superb cake to serve on its own or covered with marzipan and icing as a festive centrepiece. For extra flavour, skewer the surface of the cake and spoon over 4–5 tablespoons brandy or sherry before storing.

Pear slice with goats' cheese
This cake revives a traditional idea of combining sweet fruits and tart, tangy cheese in a comforting cake. Serve freshly baked, preferably while still slightly warm.

PREPARATION TIME: 15 minutes

COOKING TIME: 35–40 minutes

SERVES 8

175 g (6 oz) self-raising flour

1 teaspoon baking powder

75 g (3 oz) golden caster sugar

75 g (3 oz) sultanas

150 g (5 oz) dried pears, chopped

2 eggs, plus 2 yolks

100 ml (3½ fl oz) mild olive oil

150 g (5 oz) crumbly goats' cheese

Icing sugar, for dusting (optional)

1 Grease a 1 kg (2 lb) loaf tin and line the base and long sides with a strip of greaseproof paper. Sift the flour and baking powder into a bowl and stir in the sugar, sultanas and pears.

2 Beat the eggs and egg yolks with the oil and stir into the dry ingredients until well mixed.

3 Turn half the mixture into the tin, spreading it in an even layer. Crumble the cheese over the mixture and spoon over the remaining cake mixture.

4 Bake in a preheated oven, 180°C (350°F), Gas Mark 4, for 35–40 minutes or until deep golden and firm to the touch. Leave in the tin for 10 minutes, then lift out on to a wire rack to cool. Serve the pear slice plain or lightly dusted with icing sugar.

Tip Use an 18 cm (7 inch) round cake tin if you don't have a loaf tin.

Chocolate and coffee *Everyone loves a chocolate cake and the variety on offer here will satisfy even the most exacting of devotees. You will find all the classic combinations, such as a meltingly rich Chocolate Fudge Cake or the scrumptious Chocolate Chip and Banana Cake. For purists, the Very Gooey Chocolate Cake is the ultimate indulgence, dense, dark and bathed in glossy melted chocolate.*

If you are looking for something lighter, but with as much flavour as chocolate, the answer may be a coffee cake, such as the delectably airy Coffee and Walnut Cake. But beware, not all of these coffee cakes are guilt-free. The incredibly more-ish Chocolate Mocha Brownies are a chocolate and coffee taste sensation that is simply irresistible.

Chocolate ripple cake
Every time you make this cake, the fudgy marbling of plain and milk chocolate will be distributed differently – unpredictable but always delicious!

PREPARATION TIME: 20 minutes

COOKING TIME: 1 hour

SERVES 8–10

125 g (4 oz) plain chocolate

125 g (4 oz) milk chocolate

175 g (6 oz) unsalted butter, softened

175 g (6 oz) caster sugar

1 teaspoon vanilla extract

3 eggs, beaten

225 g (7½ oz) self-raising flour

1 teaspoon baking powder

2 tablespoons milk

1 Grease and line the base and sides of a 15 cm (6 inch) round cake tin. Grease the paper. Chop 25 g (1 oz) each of the plain and milk chocolate. Break up the remaining plain chocolate and melt it in a bowl with 5 g (¼ oz) of the butter, stirring frequently until smooth. Melt the remaining milk chocolate in a separate bowl with 5 g (¼ oz) of the butter.

2 Cream together the remaining butter with the sugar and vanilla extract until light and fluffy. Gradually beat in the eggs, a little at a time, adding a little flour if necessary to prevent curdling. Sift the flour and baking powder into the bowl. Add the milk and fold in.

3 Spread one-third of the cake mixture into the tin and spread with the melted plain chocolate. Spread with half the remaining cake mix, then the melted milk chocolate. Top with the remaining cake mixture, level the surface and scatter with the chopped chocolate.

4 Bake in a preheated oven, 160°C (325°F), Gas Mark 3, for about 1 hour or until a skewer inserted into the centre comes out clean. Transfer to a wire rack to cool.

White chocolate, rum and raisin teabread

This simple, comfy teabread is dotted with chunks of white chocolate and raisins. The rum adds a mildly alcoholic flavour and can be left out for an everyday family version.

PREPARATION TIME: 10 minutes

COOKING TIME: 40–45 minutes

SERVES 8

100 g (3½ oz) white chocolate

125 g (4 oz) unsalted butter, softened

75 g (3 oz) golden caster sugar, plus extra for dusting (optional)

2 eggs

150 g (5 oz) self-raising flour

1 teaspoon baking powder

3 tablespoons white or dark rum

50 g (2 oz) raisins

1 Grease and line the base and sides of a 15 cm (6 inch) square tin or 500 g (1 lb) loaf tin. Grease the paper. Using a sharp knife, shave off a quarter of the chocolate into long shards. Roughly chop the rest.

2 Put the butter, sugar, eggs, flour, baking powder and rum in a bowl and beat together until smooth and creamy.

3 Stir in the raisins and chopped chocolate and turn into the tin. Level the surface and scatter with the chocolate shards.

4 Bake in a preheated oven, 180°C (350°F), Gas Mark 4, for 40–45 minutes or until risen and golden and a skewer inserted into the centre comes out clean. Transfer to a wire rack to cool. Serve lightly dusted with caster sugar, if liked.

Chocolate fudge cake

This is a rich, claggy, chocolate-packed cake with not the faintest hint of dryness. It's great any time, from midweek indulgence to holiday treat.

PREPARATION TIME: 25 minutes, plus cooling

COOKING TIME: 20–25 minutes

SERVES 12

100 g (3½ oz) cocoa powder

100 g (3½ oz) plain chocolate, chopped

200 g (7 oz) unsalted butter, softened

325 g (11 oz) light muscovado sugar

275 g (9 oz) self-raising flour

½ teaspoon baking powder

3 eggs, beaten

Fudge icing

300 g (10 oz) plain chocolate, broken up

225 g (7½ oz) icing sugar

200 g (7 oz) unsalted butter, softened

1 Grease and base-line 3 x 20 cm (8 inch) sandwich tins. (If you only have 2 tins, bake a third of the cake mix afterwards.) Whisk the cocoa powder in a bowl with 300 ml (½ pint) boiling water until smooth. Stir in the chopped chocolate and leave to cool, stirring occasionally.

2 Beat together the butter, sugar, flour, baking powder and eggs until smooth. Beat in the chocolate mixture and divide evenly among the tins. Level the surface and bake in a preheated oven, 180°C (350°F), Gas Mark 4, for 20–25 minutes or until just firm to the touch. Transfer to a wire rack to cool.

3 Make the icing. Melt the chocolate in a small bowl. Remove from the heat and leave to cool slightly. Beat the icing sugar and butter together until creamy, then beat in the chocolate until smooth.

4 Use the icing to sandwich the cake layers on a serving plate. Pile the remainder on top, spreading it evenly with a palette knife over the top and sides.

Chocolate fudge cake

Very gooey chocolate cake

The ultimate chocolate cake – rich, dark, slightly squidgy in the middle and bathed in glossy melted chocolate. Complete the indulgence with lashings of cream.

PREPARATION TIME: 25 minutes

COOKING TIME: 40–45 minutes

SERVES 10

250 g (8 oz) plain chocolate, broken up

2 tablespoons milk

175 g (6 oz) unsalted butter, very soft

200 g (7 oz) light muscovado sugar

175 g (6 oz) ground almonds

2 tablespoons cocoa powder

40 g (1½ oz) plain flour

5 eggs, separated

Chocolate coating

15 g (½ oz) caster sugar

25 g (1 oz) unsalted butter

150 g (5 oz) plain chocolate, broken up

1 Grease and line the base and sides of a 20 cm (8 inch) round cake tin. Melt the chocolate and milk together in a large heatproof bowl.

2 Add the butter, sugar, almonds, cocoa, flour and egg yolks and beat until smooth. In a separate, thoroughly clean bowl whisk the egg whites until peaking. Use a large metal spoon to fold a quarter of the whites into the mixture to lighten it, then fold in the remainder.

3 Turn the mixture into the tin and level the surface. Bake in a preheated oven, 180°C (350°F), Gas Mark 4, for 30–35 minutes or until just firm. Leave to cool in the tin, then transfer to a serving plate.

4 Make the chocolate coating. Heat the sugar, butter and 3 tablespoons water in a small saucepan until the butter has melted and the sugar has dissolved. Remove from the heat, add the chocolate and leave until melted. Pour over the cake and store in a cool place.

Tip Avoid overcooking this cake or it will start to dry out. It is better slightly undercooked if you are not certain.

Coffee and walnut cake *Some classic cake recipes never lose their appeal, and this is one of them. The cake itself is light and airy and better for slicing if made a day in advance.*

PREPARATION TIME: 25 minutes

COOKING TIME: 25 minutes

SERVES 10

1 tablespoon instant espresso powder

175 g (6 oz) unsalted butter, softened

175 g (6 oz) light muscovado sugar

3 eggs

175 g (6 oz) self-raising flour

1 teaspoon baking powder

50 g (2 oz) walnuts, chopped

Coffee Buttercream (see page 16)

walnut halves, to decorate

1 Grease and base-line 2 x 18 cm (7 inch) sandwich tins. Dissolve the coffee in 2 teaspoons boiling water.

2 Put the butter, sugar, eggs, flour and baking powder in a bowl and beat until smooth and creamy.

3 Beat in the coffee and walnuts and divide the mixture between the tins. Level the surface and bake in a preheated oven, 180°C (350°F), Gas Mark 4, for about 25 minutes or until risen and just firm to the touch. Transfer to a wire rack to cool.

4 Sandwich the cakes together with half the buttercream and spread the top of the cake with the remainder. Decorate with walnut halves.

Iced espresso cakes

These little cupcakes are simple to make with storecupboard basics. You can use any good-quality, strongly flavoured coffee instead of espresso.

PREPARATION TIME: 15 minutes

COOKING TIME: 25 minutes

MAKES 12

2 teaspoons instant espresso powder

150 g (5 oz) unsalted butter, softened

150 g (5 oz) golden caster sugar

175 g (6 oz) self-raising flour

3 eggs

chocolate coffee beans, to decorate (optional)

Coffee icing

2 tablespoons milk

1½ teaspoons instant espresso powder

50 g (2 oz) unsalted butter

200 g (7 oz) icing sugar

1 Line a 12-section muffin tray with paper muffin cases. Blend the espresso powder with 2 teaspoons boiling water.

2 Put the butter, sugar, flour and eggs in a bowl. Add the dissolved coffee liquid and beat until smooth and creamy.

3 Divide the mixture among the cases and bake in a preheated oven, 180°C (350°F), Gas Mark 4, for 20 minutes or until risen and just firm. Transfer to a wire rack to cool.

4 Make the icing. Put the milk, coffee and butter in a small pan and heat gently until the butter has melted and the coffee has dissolved. Turn into a bowl and beat in the icing sugar. Spread over the cakes with a palette knife and decorate with coffee beans if used.

Chocolate mocha brownies

Like all the best brownie recipes, this version's both gooey and fudgy. Try to resist the temptation to over-indulge – they are packed with chocolate and incredibly rich!

PREPARATION TIME: 15 minutes

COOKING TIME: 30 minutes

MAKES 15

200 g (7 oz) milk chocolate
250 g (8 oz) plain chocolate, broken up
175 g (6 oz) unsalted butter
2 tablespoons instant coffee
3 eggs
225 g (7½ oz) light muscovado sugar
75 g (3 oz) self-raising flour
½ teaspoon baking powder

1 Grease and line a shallow 27 x 18 cm (11 x 7 inch) rectangular tin or a 23 cm (9 inch) square tin. Chop the milk chocolate into small chunks.

2 Melt the plain chocolate in a bowl with the butter, stirring frequently, until smooth. Stir in the coffee.

3 In a separate bowl beat together the eggs and sugar. Stir in the melted chocolate mixture. Sift the flour and baking powder into the bowl and stir until they are combined.

4 Add the chopped milk chocolate and turn the mixture into the tin. Level the surface and bake in a preheated oven, 190°C (375°F), Gas Mark 5, for about 30 minutes or until a crust has formed but the mixture feels quite soft underneath. Leave to cool in the tin, then serve cut into squares.

Variation Stir in 100 g (3½ oz) chopped walnuts or pecans with the milk chocolate.

Chocolate blondies
White chocolate and macadamia nuts give these cakes a much paler colour than regular brownies, hence the name. The flavour is, of course, just as chocolatey and delicious.

PREPARATION TIME: 15 minutes

COOKING TIME: 35 minutes

MAKES 15

350 g (11½ oz) white chocolate

75 g (3 oz) unsalted butter

3 eggs

125 g (4 oz) golden caster sugar

1 teaspoon vanilla extract

150 g (5 oz) self-raising flour

100 g (3½ oz) macadamia nuts, roughly chopped

1 Grease and line a shallow 27 x 18 cm (11 x 7 inch) rectangular tin or a 23 cm (9 inch) square tin. Chop 250 g (8 oz) of the chocolate into small chunks.

2 Melt the remaining chocolate in a bowl with the butter, stirring frequently, until the mixture is smooth. In a separate bowl beat together the eggs, sugar and vanilla extract until smooth. Stir in the melted chocolate mixture.

3 Add the flour and stir until combined. Stir in the chopped chocolate and nuts and turn the mixture into the tin. Level the surface and bake in a preheated oven, 190°C (375°F), Gas Mark 5, for about 30 minutes or until golden and the centre feels only just firm to the touch. Leave to cool in the tin and serve cut into squares.

Coffee and muscovado cake

This simple coffee cake is topped with buttery muscovado cream. The coffee flavour in the sponge comes from crushed chocolate coffee beans.

PREPARATION TIME: 20 minutes

COOKING TIME: 50 minutes

SERVES 10

50 g (2 oz) chocolate-covered coffee beans, plus extra to decorate

175 g (6 oz) unsalted butter, softened

175 g (6 oz) light muscovado sugar

3 eggs

175 g (6 oz) self-raising flour

1 teaspoon baking powder

Muscovado cream

125 g (4 oz) light muscovado sugar

125 g (4 oz) unsalted butter, softened

25 g (1 oz) icing sugar

1 Grease and base-line a 20 cm (8 inch) round cake tin. Put 50 g (2 oz) coffee beans in a polythene bag and crush them with a rolling pin.

2 Tip them into a bowl and add the butter, sugar, eggs, flour and baking powder. Beat until smooth and creamy. Turn the mixture into the tin and level the surface. Bake in a preheated oven, 180°C (350°F), Gas Mark 4, for about 45 minutes or until just firm to the touch. Transfer to a wire rack to cool.

3 Make the muscovado cream. Put the muscovado sugar in a small saucepan with 2 tablespoons water and heat gently until the sugar has dissolved. Remove from the heat, pour into a bowl and leave to cool.

4 Beat in the butter and icing sugar. Add a dash of boiling water and beat until light and fluffy. Spread over the cake and scatter with chocolate coffee beans.

Tip If you can't get hold of chocolate coffee beans, use 2 teaspoons of coffee powder dissolved in a tablespoon of hot water.

Zucotto

To form a good domed shape for this classic Italian speciality, use a mixing bowl with a rounded base rather than a flat one. Serve the cake cut into wedges with morning or after-dinner coffee.

PREPARATION TIME: 25 minutes, plus chilling
SERVES 6–8

350 g (11½ oz) bought or homemade chocolate sponge cake

350 ml (12 fl oz) double cream

4 tablespoons maraschino liqueur or brandy

40 g (1½ oz) icing sugar, plus extra for dusting

75 g (3 oz) plain chocolate, chopped

50 g (2 oz) whole sweet almonds, toasted and chopped

50 g (2 oz) unblanched hazelnuts, toasted and chopped

75 g (3 oz) natural glacé cherries, halved

cocoa powder, for dusting

1 Thinly slice the chocolate cake. Line a 1.8 litre (3 pint) bowl with clingfilm. Use about two-thirds of the cake to line the bowl in a single layer, cutting it to fit neatly together. The lining should come about two-thirds of the way up the sides of the bowl.

2 Put the cream, the liqueur or brandy and the icing sugar in a bowl and whisk until just peaking. Stir in the chocolate, nuts and cherries. Spoon the mixture into the cake-lined bowl, spreading it in an even layer.

3 Use the remaining cake and any excess cake lining the bowl to cover the top of the filling. Cover the bowl with clingfilm and chill overnight.

4 Invert the cake on to a plate and peel away the clingfilm. Cut 4 wedge-shaped templates from paper. Dust the cake with icing sugar and lay the templates over the top with their points meeting in the centre to make a sunburst pattern. Dust between the paper with cocoa powder, then carefully lift away the paper.

Chocolate maple stromboli *A sweet version of a classic Italian recipe that envelops delicious fillings in an enriched dough. It's packed with chocolate and hazelnuts and flavoured with maple syrup.*

PREPARATION TIME: 25 minutes, plus proving

COOKING TIME: 40 minutes

SERVES 10

2 teaspoons easy-blend dried yeast

25 g (1 oz) caster sugar, plus 1 teaspoon

150 ml (¼ pint) hand-hot milk

200 g (7 oz) plain chocolate, broken up

75 g (3 oz) salted butter, very soft

300 g (10 oz) strong bread flour

½ teaspoon ground cinnamon

100 ml (3½ fl oz) maple syrup, plus extra to serve

125 g (4 oz) unblanched hazelnuts, chopped

1 Stir the yeast and 1 teaspoon sugar into the milk in a small bowl and leave for 10 minutes or until frothy. Melt the chocolate with 25 g (1 oz) of the butter.

2 Put the flour, cinnamon and remaining sugar in a bowl. Add the yeasted milk, 50 ml (2 fl oz) of the maple syrup and the remaining butter and mix with a round-bladed knife to a soft dough, adding a little more flour if the dough feels sticky. Turn out on to a floured surface and knead for 10 minutes or until smooth and elastic. Transfer to a lightly oiled bowl, cover with clingfilm and leave to rise in a warm place for about 1 hour or until doubled in size.

3 Knock back the dough (see page 12) and roll it out on a floured surface to a 35 x 25 cm (14 x 10 inch) rectangle. Stir the remaining maple syrup into the chocolate mixture and spread to within 1 cm (½ inch) of the edges of the dough. Scatter with the nuts and loosely roll up the dough, starting from a short end. Transfer to a lightly greased baking sheet with the join underneath. Pinch the ends firmly together.

4 Cover loosely with clingfilm and leave in a warm place for 45 minutes or until risen. Pierce the dough all over and right through to the base with a skewer. Bake in a preheated oven, 200°C (400°F), Gas Mark 6, for 40 minutes or until risen and golden, covering the cake with foil if it starts to brown too much. Leave to cool before slicing and drizzling with extra maple syrup.

Chocolate chip and banana cake

This recipe uses a deliciously sweet banana and raisin purée and a generous amount of creamy white chocolate pieces, so there's no need to add any extra sugar.

PREPARATION TIME: 20 minutes

COOKING TIME: about 1 hour

SERVES 10

3 ripe bananas

250 g (8 oz) raisins

1 tablespoon lemon juice

175 g (6 oz) unsalted butter, softened

3 eggs

125 g (4 oz) self-raising flour

125 g (4 oz) wholemeal flour

1 teaspoon baking powder

250 g (9 oz) white chocolate, chopped

1 Grease and line the base and sides of a 20 cm (8 inch) round cake tin or 18 cm (7 inch) square tin. Cut the bananas into chunks and put them in a food processor with 150 g (5 oz) of the raisins and the lemon juice. Blend to a thick paste.

2 Put the butter, eggs, flours and baking powder in a bowl and beat until smooth and creamy. Stir in the purée, 150 g (5 oz) of the chopped chocolate and half the remaining raisins.

3 Turn the mixture into the tin and level the surface. Scatter with the raisins and a further 50 g (2 oz) of the chocolate. Bake the cake in a preheated oven, 160°C (325°F), Gas Mark 3, for about 1 hour or until just firm and a skewer inserted into the centre comes out clean. Transfer to a wire rack to cool.

4 Melt the remaining white chocolate in a small heatproof bowl. Using a teaspoon, scribble lines of melted chocolate over the cooled cake.

Sticky chocolate fig buns

Packed with orange-poached figs and chocolate chunks, these little buns are good enough to serve warm as a pudding or, when they are cool, as convenient little snacks.

PREPARATION TIME: 30 minutes, plus cooling

COOKING TIME: 25 minutes

MAKES 12

175 g (6 oz) dried figs, chopped

150 ml (¼ pint) freshly squeezed orange juice

100 g (3½ oz) unsalted butter, softened

125 g (4 oz) golden caster sugar

2 eggs

150 g (5 oz) self-raising flour

25 g (1 oz) cocoa powder

1 teaspoon baking powder

100 g (3½ oz) plain or milk chocolate, chopped

Glaze

100 g (3½ oz) golden caster sugar

15 g (½ oz) unsalted butter

1 Grease a 12-section muffin tray. Put the figs and orange juice in a small saucepan and heat gently until the juice starts to bubble. Cook gently, uncovered, for about 5 minutes or until the figs have plumped up and the juice is absorbed. Leave to cool.

2 Put the butter, sugar, eggs, flour, cocoa and baking powder in a bowl and beat until smooth and creamy. Stir in the chopped chocolate and fig mixture.

3 Divide the mixture among the tin sections and bake in a preheated oven, 180°C (350°F), Gas Mark 4, for 25 minutes or until risen and just firm. Leave in the tin for 5 minutes, then transfer to a wire rack to cool.

4 Meanwhile, make the glaze. Heat the sugar in a small saucepan with 4 tablespoons water until dissolved. Bring to the boil and boil rapidly for about 5 minutes or until deep golden. Plunge the base of the pan into a bowl of cold water to prevent further cooking. Add 1 tablespoon water to the syrup and return to the heat, stirring gently until smooth. Stir in the butter until melted. Brush over the buns.

Chocolate roulade with Irish coffee cream

*Soft, squidgy and full of chocolate and cream, this roulade makes a
brilliant dessert. Assemble several hours in advance so it's easier to slice.*

PREPARATION TIME: 20 minutes

COOKING TIME: 20 minutes

SERVES 8

175 g (6 oz) plain chocolate, broken up

5 eggs, separated

150 g (5 oz) golden caster sugar, plus extra
   to sprinkle

1 tablespoon instant espresso powder

200 ml (7 fl oz) double cream

4 tablespoons whisky

1 Grease and line a 33 x 23 cm (13 x 9 inch)
Swiss roll tin. Grease the paper. Melt the
chocolate in a small heatproof bowl.

2 Beat together the egg yolks and sugar for
3–4 minutes until thickened and pale.
Whisk in the melted chocolate. In a
separate, thoroughly clean bowl whisk
the egg whites until peaking. Fold a
quarter of the whites into the chocolate
mixture to lighten it, then fold in the
remainder. Turn the mixture into the tin,
spreading it gently to the corners.

3 Bake in a preheated oven, 180°C
(350°F), Gas Mark 4, for about
20 minutes or until risen and just firm.
Sprinkle a sheet of baking parchment
with caster sugar.

4 Leave the cake in the tin for 10 minutes,
then invert it on to the parchment and
peel away the lining paper. Cover with
a damp tea towel and leave to cool.

5 Blend the espresso with 1 tablespoon
boiling water to dissolve. Put it in a bowl
with the cream and whisky and whisk
until just peaking. Spread the cream
almost to the edges of the roulade and
roll up, starting from a short end. Turn
on to a serving plate.

Liqueur drizzled coffee cake
Use percolator coffee to give this cake its stunning bands of coffee and almond flavouring. If you are using instant coffee, you should reduce the amount to 4 teaspoons.

PREPARATION TIME: 15 minutes

COOKING TIME: 45 minutes

SERVES 8

2 tablespoons espresso coffee powder

50 g (2 oz) ground almonds

50 g (2 oz) dark muscovado sugar

150 g (5 oz) golden caster sugar, plus 1 tablespoon

175 g (6 oz) unsalted butter, softened

3 eggs

200 g (7 oz) self-raising flour

1 teaspoon baking powder

50 g (2 oz) flaked almonds

½ teaspoon ground cinnamon

4 tablespoons coffee liqueur

1 Grease and line the base and sides of an 18 cm (7 inch) spring-form tin or loose-based cake tin. Grease the paper. Mix together the coffee powder, ground almonds and dark muscovado sugar.

2 Put 150 g (5 oz) caster sugar in a bowl with the butter, eggs, flour and baking powder and beat until smooth and creamy. Spread one-third into the tin and scatter with half the coffee mixture. Gently spread with half the remaining sponge mixture and scatter with the remaining coffee mixture. Finally, spread with the remaining sponge mixture.

3 Toss the remaining tablespoon of sugar with the flaked almonds and cinnamon and scatter over the surface. Bake in a preheated oven, 180°C (350°F), Gas Mark 4, for 45 minutes until just firm and a skewer inserted into the centre comes out clean. Leave in the tin for 10 minutes, then transfer to a wire rack to cool. Drizzle with the coffee liqueur before serving.

Chocolate cherry cake

Sandwiched and topped with white chocolate ganache, this cake makes a lighter alternative to the more familiar dark chocolate and cherry combination.

PREPARATION TIME: 30 minutes

COOKING TIME: 25 minutes

SERVES 8–10

4 eggs

100 g (3½ oz) caster sugar

1 teaspoon vanilla extract

100 g (3½ oz) plain flour

75 g (3 oz) white chocolate, grated

To decorate

400 g (13 oz) red or black cherries, pitted

White Chocolate Ganache (see page 19)

chocolate curls

1 Grease and base-line 2 x 18 cm (7 inch) sandwich tins. Put the eggs, sugar and vanilla extract in a large heatproof bowl over a pan of hot water and whisk for 6–8 minutes or until the whisk leaves a trail when lifted from the bowl. Remove from the heat and whisk for a further 2 minutes.

2 Sift the flour into the bowl and sprinkle with the grated chocolate. Fold in gently using a large metal spoon. Divide the mixture between the tins and gently level the surface. Bake in a preheated oven, 180°C (350°F), Gas Mark 4, for about 25 minutes or until just firm to the touch. Transfer to a wire rack to cool.

3 Halve 200 g (7 oz) of the cherries. Spread one cake layer with half the ganache and arrange the halved cherries on top. Cover with the other cake and spread with the remaining ganache. Scatter with the remaining cherries and chocolate curls.

Tip Use a vegetable peeler to pare off curls from a chocolate bar. If the chocolate is too brittle, warm it very slightly in the microwave and try again.

Chocolate fridge cake

As delicious as it is filling, this isn't the sort of cake you'd serve in chunky slices. Rich and intensely chocolatey it's a treat cut into small pieces and served with coffee.

PREPARATION TIME: 10 minutes, plus chilling

SERVES 10

300 g (10 oz) plain chocolate, broken up

75 g (3 oz) unsalted butter

125 g (4 oz) bought or homemade shortbread biscuits

125 g (4 oz) whole mixed nuts, such as almonds, hazelnuts and Brazil nuts

150 g (5 oz) milk chocolate caramel bar, broken into sections

1 Line a dampened 500 g (1 lb) loaf tin with clingfilm. Melt the plain chocolate with the butter, stirring frequently, and leave until cool but not beginning to harden.

2 Break the biscuits into small pieces. Stir the biscuits, nuts and caramel bar into the melted mixture until combined.

3 Turn into the tin and pack down in an even layer. Chill for several hours, or overnight until set.

4 To serve, lift away the tin and let the cake soften a little at room temperature so it's easier to slice. Peel away the clingfilm and serve in small pieces.

Small cakes *The charm of a small cake is that you get to eat all of it yourself. On offer here is possibly the greatest range of flavours and textures, from the gorgeous Sticky Ginger Cakes to Crumbly Raspberry and Oat Slices, which contrast tangy fruit with crunchy crumble. For a gift, try individually wrapped Baby Panettones, or a box of shell-shaped French Madeleines.*

Some of these small cakes are also among the easiest to make. Rock Buns can be whizzed up at a moment's notice, and Passionfruit and Coconut Cupcakes show how exciting the humble cupcake can be. Bear in mind, however, that these simple cakes are only at their best when absolutely fresh.

Sticky ginger cakes

Take care not to overcook these little cakes or they will lose their lovely stickiness. If you like iced ginger cakes, spread them with a little glacé icing instead of the syrup.

PREPARATION TIME: 15 minutes

COOKING TIME: 30 minutes

MAKES 8

225 g (7½ oz) plain flour

1½ teaspoons bicarbonate of soda

2 teaspoons ground ginger

125 g (4 oz) dark muscovado sugar

75 g (3 oz) unsalted butter

150 g (5 oz) black treacle

125 ml (4 fl oz) milk

2 pieces stem ginger, 30 g (1½ oz) in total, roughly chopped, plus a little syrup from the jar

1 egg, beaten

1 Grease 8 individual loaf tins, each with a 200 ml (7 fl oz) capacity. Sift the flour, bicarbonate of soda and ginger into a bowl.

2 Put the sugar, butter and treacle in a small saucepan and heat gently until the butter melts. Remove from the heat and add the milk, stem ginger and then the egg.

3 Pour the mixture over the dry ingredients and whisk until combined. Turn the mixture into the prepared tins and bake in a preheated oven, 160°C (325°F), Gas Mark 3, for about 25 minutes or until just firm.

4 Leave to cool in the tins, loosen the edges with a knife and turn out. Serve brushed with a little stem ginger syrup.

Turkish delight slice

Although Turkish delight is something of an acquired taste, these sugar-dusted morsels are bound to convert a few newcomers to its exotic flavour.

PREPARATION TIME: 20 minutes

COOKING TIME: 30–35 minutes

SERVES 12

200 g (7 oz) rose-flavoured Turkish delight

175 g (6 oz) unsalted butter, softened

125 g (4 oz) caster sugar

1 teaspoon almond extract

3 eggs, beaten

175 g (6 oz) self-raising flour

40 g (1½ oz) slivered or flaked almonds

icing sugar, for dusting

1 Grease and line the base and sides of a shallow, 20 cm (8 inch) square baking tin. Grease the paper. Chop the Turkish delight into small pieces (this is most easily done with scissors).

2 Cream together the butter and sugar until light and fluffy. Stir in the almond extract. Gradually beat in the eggs, a little at a time, beating well after each addition. Add a little of the flour if the mixture starts to curdle.

3 Sift the flour over the bowl and scatter with half the chopped Turkish delight. Using a large metal spoon, fold the ingredients together until just combined. Turn the mixture into the tin and level the surface.

4 Scatter with the remaining Turkish delight and the almonds. Bake in a preheated oven, 180°C (350°F), Gas Mark 4, for 30–35 minutes or until golden and just firm to the touch. Leave to cool in the tin. Dust with icing sugar and serve cut into fingers.

Crumbly raspberry and oat slices
Just like a dessert crumble, these little cakes provide that delicious contrast between crispy chunks of crumble and bursts of tangy fruit.

PREPARATION TIME: 15 minutes

COOKING TIME: 1 hour

MAKES 12–14 fingers

100 g (3½ oz) plain flour

75 g (3 oz) plain wholemeal flour

175 g (6 oz) porridge oats

175 g (6 oz) butter, slightly softened

150 g (5 oz) golden caster sugar

finely grated rind of 1 lemon

250 g (8 oz) fresh or frozen raspberries

icing sugar, for dusting

1 Lightly butter the base and sides of a shallow, 27 x 18 cm (10½ x 7 inch) rectangular baking tin or a similar sized roasting tin. Put the flours and oats in a bowl. Cut the butter into small pieces, add it to the dry ingredients and work with your fingers until the mixture makes a coarse crumble.

2 Stir in the sugar and lemon rind and continue to crumble the mixture together until it starts to cling together.

3 Turn half the mixture into the tin and pat it down into an even layer. Scatter the raspberries on top and sprinkle with the remaining crumble mixture.

4 Bake in a preheated oven, 180°C (350°F), Gas Mark 4, for about 1 hour or until the topping is turning golden. Cut into fingers and leave to cool in the tin. Serve dusted with icing sugar.

Rock buns
These are quick and easy to whiz up and lovely when eaten freshly baked. Don't let them hang around for too long though, or they will live up to their inappropriate name.

PREPARATION TIME: 10 minutes

COOKING TIME: 15 minutes

MAKES 20

125 g (4 oz) unsalted butter, softened

100 g (3½ oz) golden caster sugar

225 g (7½ oz) self-raising flour

1 teaspoon ground ginger

1 teaspoon ground cinnamon

1 egg, beaten

150 ml (¼ pint) milk

100 g (3½ oz) sultanas

75 g (3 oz) currants

50 g (2 oz) white sugar cubes

1 Grease 2 baking sheets. Cream together the butter and sugar until light and fluffy. Stir in the flour, spices, egg and milk and mix to a soft dough. Stir the dried fruits into the mixture.

2 Place dessertspoonfuls of the mixture on to the baking sheets, spacing them slightly apart.

3 Put the sugar cubes in a polythene bag and lightly crush with a rolling pin. Scatter over the buns and bake in a preheated oven, 190°C (375°F), Gas Mark 5, for about 15 minutes or until risen and golden. Transfer to a wire rack to cool.

Passionfruit and coconut cupcakes

Basic cupcakes are perfect vehicles for flavour variations. These coconut ones, lavishly piled up with passionfruit cream, are ideally eaten absolutely fresh.

PREPARATION TIME: 20 minutes

COOKING TIME: 20–25 minutes

MAKES 12

50 g (2 oz) creamed coconut, chilled

150 g (5 oz) unsalted butter, softened

150 g (5 oz) caster sugar

175 g (6 oz) self-raising flour

1 teaspoon baking powder

3 eggs

1 teaspoon vanilla extract

Topping

2 passionfruit

100 g (3½ oz) Greek yogurt

40 g (1½ oz) icing sugar, plus extra for dusting

150 ml (¼ pint) double or whipping cream

1 Line a 12-section muffin tray with paper muffin cases. Finely grate the creamed coconut. Put the butter, sugar, flour, baking powder, eggs and vanilla extract in a bowl and beat for 1–2 minutes or until light and creamy.

2 Whisk in the creamed coconut and divide the mixture among the paper cases. Bake in a preheated oven, 180°C (350°F), Gas Mark 4, for 20–25 minutes or until risen and just firm to the touch. Transfer to a wire rack to cool.

3 Halve the passionfruit and scoop out the pulp into a bowl. Add the yogurt, icing sugar and cream and whip until the cream is only just holding its shape.

4 Using a small sharp knife, slice a little 'lid' off each cupcake. Pile up the cream and position the lid on top. Serve dusted with icing sugar.

Baby panettones

We usually see beautifully boxed panettone breads hanging in delicatessens, particularly during the festive season. Once cooled, these mini versions look lovely rewrapped in fresh paper.

PREPARATION TIME: 25 minutes, plus proving
COOKING TIME: 20–25 minutes
MAKES 8

2 teaspoons easy-blend dried yeast

125 g (4 oz) caster sugar, plus 1 teaspoon

175 ml (6 fl oz) hand-hot milk

700 g (1 lb 6 oz) strong bread flour

4 large eggs, plus 2 yolks

2 teaspoons vanilla extract

finely grated rind of 2 lemons

175 g (6 oz) salted butter, very soft

175 g (6 oz) mixed dried fruit

1 Grease 8 x 400 ml (14 fl oz) clean food cans and line the sides with greaseproof paper. Grease the paper. Stir the yeast and 1 teaspoon sugar into the milk in a large, warm bowl and leave for 10 minutes or until frothy. Stir in 100 g (3½ oz) of the flour. Cover with clingfilm and leave for 30 minutes.

2 Add the eggs and yolks, the remaining flour and sugar, and the vanilla extract, lemon rind and butter, cut into small pieces. Mix well with a round-bladed knife to make a soft dough, adding a little more flour if the dough feels sticky. Turn out on to a lightly floured surface and knead until smooth and elastic. Transfer to a lightly oiled bowl, cover with clingfilm and leave to rise for 2–4 hours or until doubled in size.

3 Knock back the dough (see page 12) and knead in the fruit. Cut into 8 pieces and drop into the tins. Cover and leave to rise until the dough almost reaches the rims.

4 Bake in a preheated oven, 200°C (400°F), Gas Mark 6, for 20–25 minutes or until risen and golden. Leave for 5 minutes, then cool on a wire rack.

Baby panettones

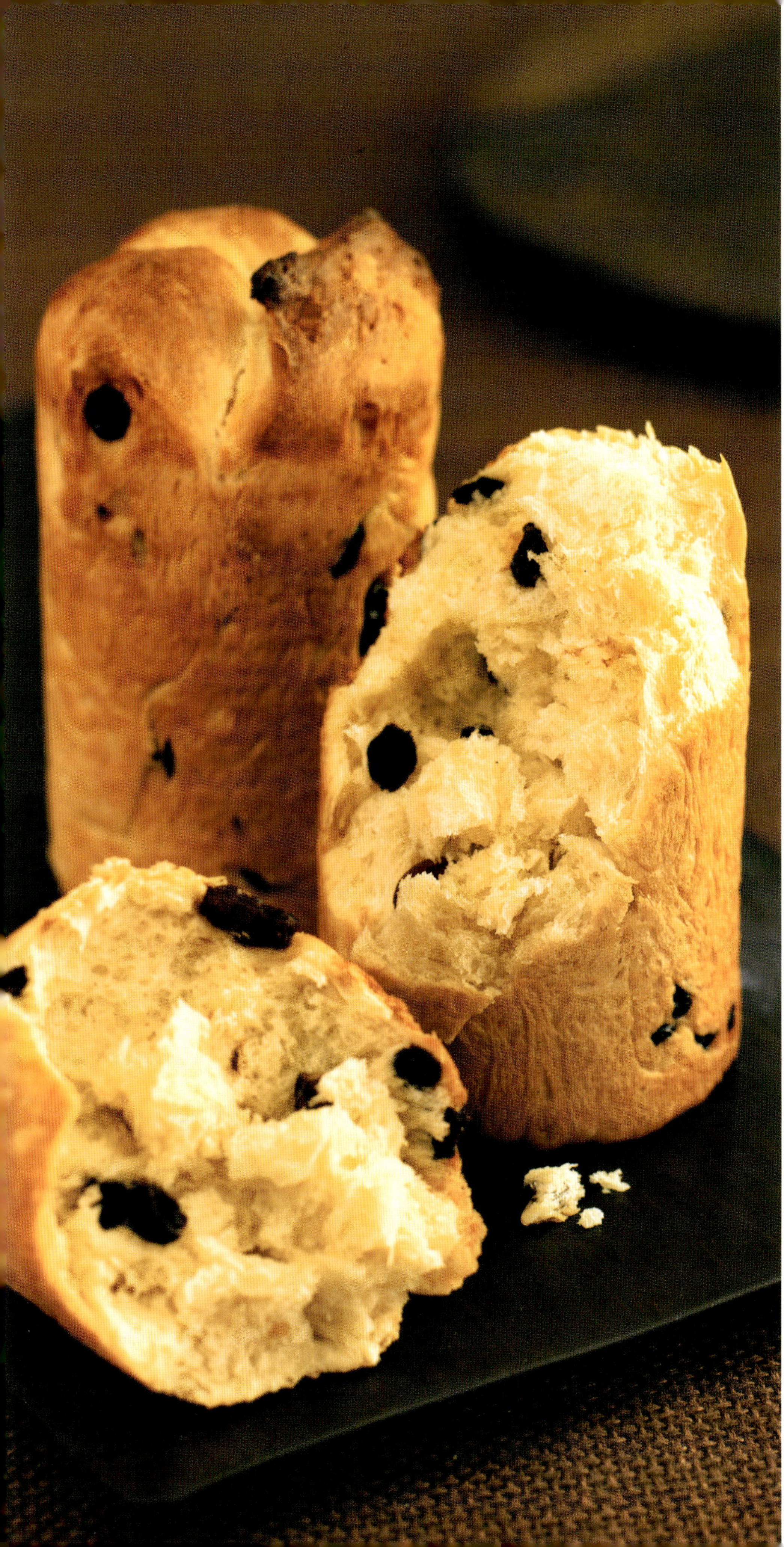

Spiced gooseberry buns

Lining the sections of a muffin tray with squares of paper is a great alternative to paper cake cases, but you can use the ready-made ones if you want to get cooking quickly.

PREPARATION TIME: 20 minutes

COOKING TIME: 25 minutes

MAKES 12

300 g (10 oz) gooseberries

175 g (6 oz) unsalted butter, softened

150 g (5 oz) golden caster sugar

3 eggs

100 g (3½ oz) self-raising flour, plus 1 teaspoon

100 g (3½ oz) oatmeal

1 teaspoon baking powder

½ teaspoon ground allspice

2 tablespoons demerara sugar

1 Cut out 12 squares of greaseproof paper, each 13 x 13 cm (5½ x 5½ inches), and press them into a 12-section muffin tray, creasing the folds to fit. (Don't worry if they don't stay in position – the weight of the cake mixture will hold them down when they are filled.) Reserve 150 g (5 oz) of the smallest gooseberries and halve the remainder.

2 Put the butter, sugar, eggs, 100 g (3½ oz) of the flour, oatmeal, baking powder and allspice in a bowl and beat until the mixture is smooth and creamy. Stir in the halved gooseberries.

3 Divide the mixture among the paper cases. Toss the remaining gooseberries in the teaspoon of flour and scatter them over the cake mixture.

4 Bake in a preheated oven, 180°C (350°F), Gas Mark 4, for 25 minutes or until risen and just firm. Sprinkle with the demerara sugar and transfer to a wire rack to cool.

French madeleines

You will need shell-shaped madeleine moulds for these little cakes. They are just the right size for small sponges that are crisp and biscuity at the edges and soft and airy in the middle.

PREPARATION TIME: 25 minutes

COOKING TIME: 10–12 minutes

MAKES 18–20

125 g (4 oz) self-raising flour, plus extra for dusting

3 eggs

125 g (4 oz) caster sugar

finely grated rind of 1 lemon

½ teaspoon baking powder

125 g (4 oz) unsalted butter, melted

icing sugar, for dusting

1 Grease the sections of two madeleine trays with melted butter and dust with flour, tapping out the excess.

2 Whisk together the eggs, sugar and lemon rind until thick and pale and the whisk leaves a thin trail when lifted from the bowl.

3 Sift the flour and baking powder into the bowl and gently fold in using a large metal spoon. Drizzle the butter around the edges of the mixture and fold in until just combined.

4 Divide the mixture among the moulds, making each about two-thirds full. Bake in a preheated oven, 220°C (425°F), Gas Mark 7, for 10–12 minutes or until risen and deep golden. Leave for 5 minutes, then ease the cakes out of the moulds with a palette knife and cool on a wire rack. Serve dusted with icing sugar.

Cinnamon doughnuts

As long as you eat these freshly cooked, their flavour and texture far exceed the best bought versions – impossible to eat without licking your lips!

PREPARATION TIME: 25 minutes, plus proving

COOKING TIME: about 15 minutes

MAKES 12

2 teaspoons easy-blend dried yeast

75 g (3 oz) caster sugar, plus 1 teaspoon

400 g (13 oz) strong bread flour

1 egg, beaten

50 g (2 oz) lightly salted butter, melted

100 ml (3½ fl oz) hand-hot milk

To finish

½ teaspoon ground cinnamon

100 g (3½ oz) caster sugar

vegetable oil, for frying

1 Stir the yeast and 1 teaspoon sugar into 100 ml (3½ fl oz) hand-hot water in a small bowl and leave to stand for 10 minutes or until frothy. Mix the flour with the remaining sugar in a large bowl. Add the egg, butter, milk and yeasted mixture and mix to a dough.

2 Knead gently on a floured surface for 10 minutes or until smooth and elastic. Put in a lightly oiled bowl, cover with clingfilm and leave in a warm place for about 1 hour or until doubled in size.

3 Knock back the dough (see page 12) and divide into 12 equal pieces. Roll each into a ball and space well apart, on 2 lightly oiled baking sheets. Cover loosely with oiled clingfilm and leave to rise for about 40 minutes or until doubled in size.

4 Mix the cinnamon on a plate with the sugar. Heat 8 cm (3 inches) oil in a large, heavy-based saucepan until a small piece of bread starts to brown in 30 seconds. Fry the doughnuts, a few at a time, for 2–3 minutes or until puffed and golden. Drain with a slotted spoon and dry on kitchen paper. Toss in cinnamon sugar.

Pistachio and honey buns
Use a well-flavoured honey in these buns or the flavour might not be noticeable enough. They make quick and easy little treats, best served freshly baked.

PREPARATION TIME: 15 minutes

COOKING TIME: 15–20 minutes

MAKES 12

350 g (11½ oz) plain flour

1 tablespoon baking powder

100 g (3½ oz) pistachio nuts, skinned and roughly chopped

75 g (3 oz) raisins

50 g (2 oz) golden caster sugar

150 g (5 oz) strong-flavoured, clear honey, plus extra to serve

2 eggs, beaten

1 tablespoon lemon juice

125 ml (4 fl oz) milk

75 g (3 oz) unsalted butter, melted

1 Grease a 12-section, nonstick muffin tray (see tip). Sift the flour and baking powder into a bowl and stir in the nuts, raisins and sugar.

2 Mix together the honey, eggs, lemon juice, milk and butter and add to the bowl. Stir the ingredients gently together until only just combined.

3 Divide the mixture among the tin sections and bake in a preheated oven, 200°C (400°F), Gas Mark 6, for 15–20 minutes or until risen and just firm. Transfer to a wire rack to cool and serve drizzled with extra honey.

Tip If you don't have a nonstick muffin tray, line the tray sections with paper muffin cases.

Lavender loaves
Make these little treats in summer when the lavender flowers have just opened. At this stage they can also be frozen for later use.

PREPARATION TIME: 20 minutes

COOKING TIME: 20–25 minutes

MAKES 8

1 tablespoon lavender flowers (about 8 flowerheads), plus extra to decorate

175 g (6 oz) unsalted butter, softened

175 g (6 oz) golden caster sugar

3 eggs

175 g (6 oz) self-raising flour

1 teaspoon baking powder

finely grated rind of 1 lemon

Glacé Icing (see page 16)

lilac food colouring

1 Grease 8 individual loaf tins, each with a 200 ml (7 fl oz) capacity. Line the bases and long sides with strips of paper. Grease the paper.

2 Put half the lavender flowers in a bowl with the butter, sugar, eggs, flour, baking powder and lemon rind and beat until smooth and creamy.

3 Divide the mixture among the prepared tins. Bake in a preheated oven, 180°C (350°F), Gas Mark 4, for 20–25 minutes or until risen and just firm. Transfer to a wire rack to cool.

4 Stir the reserved lavender flowers and a dash of food colouring into the icing. Spoon over the icing, and decorate with extra flowers.

Honey and walnut cakes

These little cakes are best eaten the day they are made. If you don't want to line individual dishes, use a 20 cm (8 inch) round tin instead, allowing a little more cooking time.

PREPARATION TIME: 20 minutes, plus cooling

COOKING TIME: 20–25 minutes

MAKES 8

150 ml (¼ pint) double cream

2 sprigs of rosemary, plus extra small sprigs for decoration

125 g (4 oz) broken walnuts

2 tablespoons cornflour

175 g (6 oz) clear honey

2 teaspoons lemon juice

2 eggs, beaten

150 ml (¼ pint) buttermilk

65 g (2½ oz) unsalted butter, melted

125 g (4 oz) instant polenta

½ teaspoon baking powder

25 g (1 oz) golden caster sugar

1 Grease and base-line 8 ramekin dishes, each with 125 ml (4 fl oz) capacity, or sit 8 x 8 cm (3 inch) metal rings on a baking sheet and line the base and sides of each.

2 Put the cream in a small saucepan with the rosemary and heat gently until hot and beginning to bubble around the edges. Pour into a bowl and leave to cool. Roughly chop 15 g (½ oz) of the walnuts and reserve. Grind the remainder in a food processor with the cornflour.

3 Beat together the honey, lemon juice, eggs, buttermilk and butter. Put the ground walnuts, polenta, baking powder and sugar in a bowl. Add the honey mixture and mix to a thick, smooth paste. Divide among the dishes. Bake in a preheated oven, 180°C (350°F), Gas Mark 4, for 20–25 minutes or until just firm. Leave in the moulds for 10 minutes before turning out.

4 Lift the rosemary sprigs from the cream and whip the cream until peaking. Spread the cream over the cakes and serve decorated with the chopped walnuts and small rosemary sprigs.

Candied fruit and fig cakes

For maximum flavour use good-quality candied peel, which often comes in large pieces. Ideally, serve these little cakes warm with dollops of soft, creamy mascarpone.

PREPARATION TIME: 20 minutes, plus soaking

COOKING TIME: 20 minutes

SERVES 6

100 g (3½ oz) candied peel, chopped

3 tablespoons Cointreau or other orange-flavoured liqueur

3 figs

1 tablespoon lemon juice

100 g (3½ oz) clear honey, plus 4 tablespoons

125 g (4 oz) unsalted butter, softened

2 eggs

125 g (4 oz) self-raising flour

½ teaspoon baking powder

1 Put the candied peel and liqueur in a small bowl and leave them to soak for 1 hour. Grease 6 loaf tins, each with a 200 ml (7 fl oz) capacity, and line the bases and long sides with strips of greaseproof paper.

2 Thinly slice the figs and lay 3 slices in the base of each tin. Chop any remaining figs. Mix the lemon juice and 2 tablespoons honey, and spoon over the figs.

3 Tip the candied peel and any unabsorbed liqueur into a food processor and blend to a paste. Add the 100 g (3½ oz) honey, butter, eggs, flour and baking powder and blend again until smooth, scraping the mixture down from the sides of the bowl if necessary. (The mixture might look slightly curdled at this stage.) Stir in the chopped figs.

4 Divide the mixture among the tins and level the tops. Bake in a preheated oven, 180°C (350°F), Gas Mark 4, for about 20 minutes or until just firm to the touch. Leave to cool slightly in the tins, then invert on to plates. Serve warm or cold, drizzled with the remaining honey.

Special occasions *When you really want to impress, here are some truly extravagant and unusual cakes for special occasions. These are the cakes that call for fresh fruits at the peak of their seasonal perfection, smothered in lashings of double cream. Some recipes are enriched versions of the classics, such as the Strawberry Shortcake laced with Cointreau and mascarpone cream, while others, such as the luscious French Chestnut Torte, with its topping of caramelized chestnuts, or the juicy Mango and Coconut Cake, partnered with lime syrup and rum, offer a chance to sample new combinations of flavours. For something really adventurous, try the Chilli and Pineapple Torte, speckled with red chilli and drizzled with vodka syrup. Each one of these mouthwatering cakes is sheer indulgence!*

Mango and coconut cake

Use very ripe mangoes for this cake, to provide a sweet juicy contrast to the tangy lime syrup. Rum is a natural partner for lime, but vodka or tequila would work just as well.

PREPARATION TIME: 30 minutes, plus cooling

COOKING TIME: 30–35 minutes

SERVES 10–12

50 g (2 oz) creamed coconut, chilled

150 g (5 oz) unsalted butter, softened

150 g (5 oz) caster sugar

175 g (6 oz) self-raising flour

1 teaspoon baking powder

3 eggs

1 teaspoon vanilla extract

To finish

75 g (3 oz) caster sugar

finely grated rind and juice of 3 limes

5 tablespoons white rum

300 ml (½ pint) extra thick double cream

2 medium mangoes, thinly sliced

icing sugar, for dusting

toasted coconut shavings, to decorate

1 Grease and line the base and sides of a 23 cm (9 inch) round cake tin. Grease the paper. Finely grate the creamed coconut. Put the butter, sugar, flour, baking powder, eggs and vanilla extract in a bowl and beat until smooth and creamy. Stir in the coconut.

2 Turn the mixture into the tin, level the surface and bake in a preheated oven, 180°C (350°F), Gas Mark 4, for 25–30 minutes or until just firm. Transfer to a wire rack to cool.

3 To finish the cake, heat the sugar in a small saucepan with 100 ml (3½ fl oz) water until the sugar dissolves. Heat gently for 3 minutes, then leave to cool.

4 Split the cake into three horizontal layers. Stir the lime rind, juice and rum into the syrup. Drizzle 3 tablespoonfuls of the liquid over each cake.

5 Whip the cream with the remaining syrup until it holds its shape. Sandwich the cakes with the mango slices and cream and dust the top generously with icing sugar. Scatter with toasted coconut shavings.

Peach and almond roulade

Make this gorgeous roulade when peaches are juicy and at their absolute best. Leave slightly under-ripe ones in the fruit bowl for a couple of days to accelerate ripening.

PREPARATION TIME: 20 minutes, plus chilling

COOKING TIME: 20 minutes

SERVES 8

125 g (4 oz) white almond paste

5 eggs, separated

125 g (4 oz) caster sugar, plus extra for dusting

3 tablespoons plain flour

2 tablespoons brandy or almond liqueur

2 ripe peaches

300 g (10 oz) crème fraîche

1 Grease and line a 33 x 23 cm (13 x 9 inch) Swiss roll tin with baking parchment. Grease the paper. Grate the almond paste.

2 Whisk the egg yolks in a bowl with the sugar until pale and creamy. Whisk in the almond paste. Stir in the flour.

3 In a separate, thoroughly clean bowl whisk the egg whites until peaking. Use a large metal spoon to fold the egg whites into the almond mixture until combined. Turn the mixture into the tin and spread it gently into the corners.

4 Bake in a preheated oven, 180°C (350°F), Gas Mark 4, for 20 minutes or until risen and firm to the touch. Sprinkle a sheet of baking parchment with sugar and invert the roulade on to it. Leave to cool.

5 Drizzle the liqueur over the sponge. Thinly slice the peaches. Spread the crème fraîche over the sponge and scatter with the peaches. Starting at a thin end, roll up the roulade and transfer to a serving plate. Chill until ready to serve.

Strawberry shortcake

Laced with mascarpone-enriched cream and liqueur, this recipe makes a more extravagant strawberry shortcake than many versions. It's perfect for tea in the garden.

PREPARATION TIME: 25 minutes

COOKING TIME: about 35 minutes

SERVES 8

175 g (6 oz) unsalted butter, softened

100 g (3½ oz) caster sugar

2 eggs, beaten

2 teaspoons vanilla extract

225 g (7½ oz) self-raising flour

1 teaspoon baking powder

250 g (8 oz) strawberries

100 g (3½ oz) raspberries

3 tablespoons Cointreau or other orange-flavoured liqueur

6 tablespoons redcurrant jelly

250 g (8 oz) mascarpone cheese

300 ml (½ pint) double cream

1 Grease an 18 cm (7 inch) round cake tin. Cream together the butter and sugar until light and fluffy. Gradually beat in the eggs and vanilla extract. Sift the flour and baking powder into the bowl and stir until combined. Turn into the tin and level the surface. Bake in a preheated oven, 180°C (350°F), Gas Mark 4, for 30 minutes or until just firm to the touch. Transfer to a wire rack to cool.

2 Halve the strawberries and mix them in a bowl with the raspberries and 1 tablespoon liqueur. Cut the cake in half horizontally.

3 Melt the redcurrant jelly in a saucepan with 1 tablespoon water. Beat the mascarpone with the cream and remaining liqueur until peaking. Spread the base of the cake with half the mascarpone cream and scatter with half the fruits. Brush with half the jelly and top with the remaining cake.

4 Finish the top with the remaining cream, fruits and jelly and serve.

Pannacotta and pine nut torte

This recipe combines creamy pannacotta with layers of airy whisked sponge. If you are making it a day in advance, reduce the quantity of gelatine to 1 teaspoon.

PREPARATION TIME: 30 minutes, plus cooling and chilling

COOKING TIME: 25–30 minutes

SERVES 10

100 g (3½ oz) caster sugar

4 eggs

100 g (3½ oz) plain flour

50 g (2 oz) unsalted butter, melted

To finish

1½ teaspoons powdered gelatine

400 g (13 oz) mascarpone cheese

5 tablespoons lemon juice

125 g (4 oz) caster sugar

300 ml (½ pint) double cream

100 g (3½ oz) pine nuts, toasted

icing sugar, for dusting

1 Grease and line the base and sides of a 20 cm (8 inch) loose-based cake tin. Grease the paper. Place the sugar and eggs in a large heatproof bowl over a pan of hot water and whisk for 6–8 minutes or until the whisk leaves a trail when lifted from the bowl. Remove the bowl from the heat and whisk for a further 2 minutes.

2 Sift half the flour into the bowl and use a large metal spoon to fold it in. Pour the cooled butter around the edges of the mixture and sift in the remaining flour. Fold the ingredients together and turn the mixture into the tin, spreading it gently to the edges. Bake in a preheated oven, 190°C (375°F), Gas Mark 5, for 20–25 minutes or until just firm to the touch. Transfer to a wire rack to cool. Reline the sides of the tin with a strip of baking parchment.

3 Sprinkle the gelatine over 3 tablespoons water in a small bowl. Put the mascarpone in a saucepan with the lemon juice and sugar and heat until smooth. When very hot and bubbling around the edges, remove from the heat and stir in the gelatine until completely dissolved. Turn into a bowl and stir in the cream and three-quarters of the pine nuts.

4 Cut the cake in half horizontally and place one layer back in the relined tin. Reserve a ladleful of the mascarpone mixture and pour the remainder over the sponge so it runs down the sides of the sponge to fill any gap between sponge and tin. Press the second cake layer over the top, cut side face down, until the mascarpone mixture is visible around the edges. Spread the reserved mixture on top and scatter with the reserved pine nuts. Chill for several hours or overnight until lightly set. Remove from the tin and serve dusted with icing sugar.

French chestnut torte

Like many cakes that use whisked egg whites, this one will sink slightly in the middle after baking, making a perfect case for the syrupy chestnuts.

PREPARATION TIME: 25 minutes

COOKING TIME: 45 minutes

SERVES 8

75 g (3 oz) sultanas

3 tablespoons brandy or rum

350 g (11½ oz) unsweetened chestnut purée

50 g (2 oz) unsalted butter, softened

3 eggs, separated

125 g (4 oz) golden caster sugar

65 g (2½ oz) plain flour

Caramelized chestnuts

75 g (3 oz) golden caster sugar

200 g (7 oz) peeled and cooked chestnuts, halved and toasted

crème fraîche, to serve

1 Grease and line the base and sides of a 20 cm (8 inch) round spring-form tin or a loose-based cake tin. Grease the paper. Put the sultanas in a small saucepan with 2 tablespoons of the liqueur and heat gently for 2 minutes. Beat the chestnut purée in a bowl with the butter, egg yolks, 100 g (3½ oz) of the sugar and the flour. Stir in the sultanas and any unabsorbed liqueur.

2 Whisk the egg whites in a thoroughly clean bowl until peaking. Gradually whisk in the remaining sugar.

3 Fold a quarter of the egg whites into the chestnut mixture to lighten it, then fold in the remainder. Turn the mixture into the tin and spread it gently to the edges. Bake in a preheated oven, 180°C (350°F), Gas Mark 4, for 35 minutes or until just firm. Leave in the tin to cool.

4 To caramelize the chestnuts, heat the sugar in a small, heavy-based saucepan with 4 tablespoons water until the sugar has dissolved. Bring to the boil and let the syrup bubble until it is pale golden. Stir in the remaining liqueur and the chestnuts, heating gently until the syrup is smooth. Spoon over the cake and serve warm or cold with crème fraîche.

Tip To toast the chestnuts, heat under a preheated grill, turning once, for 2–3 minutes until lightly toasted.

Chilli and pineapple torte

This buttery sponge is specked with red chilli and drizzled with vodka syrup after baking, giving a flavour that's far from predictable. A cake for adventurous cooks.

PREPARATION TIME: 25 minutes

COOKING TIME: 1 hour 5 minutes

SERVES 8–10

1 large, medium-strength red chilli, deseeded and thinly sliced

175 g (6 oz) unsalted butter, softened

275 g (9 oz) caster sugar

3 eggs

275 g (9 oz) self-raising flour

1 teaspoon baking powder

125 g (4 oz) dried pineapple, chopped

½ small fresh pineapple

6 tablespoons vodka

1 Grease and line the base and sides of a 23 cm (9 inch) round cake tin. Grease the paper. Put half the chilli in a bowl with the butter, 175 g (6 oz) of the sugar, the eggs, flour and baking powder and beat until smooth and creamy.

2 Stir in the dried pineapple pieces, turn the mixture into the tin and level the surface of the cake.

3 Cut away the skin and core from the fresh pineapple and thinly slice the flesh. Arrange the slices over the mixture with the reserved chilli. Bake in a preheated oven, 180°C (350°F), Gas Mark 4, for 1 hour or until just firm and a skewer inserted into the centre comes out clean. Transfer to a wire rack.

4 Meanwhile, put the remaining sugar in a saucepan with 4 tablespoons water and heat gently until the sugar dissolves. Bring to the boil and boil for about 5 minutes until thickened and syrupy.

5 Pierce the surface of the warm cake all over with a skewer and drizzle with half the vodka. Stir the remaining vodka into the syrup and drizzle over the surface.

Raspberry and amaretti layer cake *To make slicing easier, make the almondy sponge a day before assembling the cake so that it's got time to firm up.*

PREPARATION TIME: 40 minutes

COOKING TIME: 25 minutes

SERVES 10–12

125 g (4 oz) amaretti biscuits

5 eggs

100 g (3½ oz) caster sugar

125 g (4 oz) plain flour

175 ml (6 fl oz) Disaronno or other almond liqueur

500 g (1 lb) mascarpone cheese

50 g (2 oz) icing sugar, plus extra for dusting

300 ml (½ pint) double cream

400 g (13 oz) fresh raspberries

1 Grease and base-line 2 x 20 cm (8 inch) sandwich tins. Put the biscuits in a polythene bag and crush them with a rolling pin. Beat the eggs and sugar in a heatproof bowl over a pan of hot water until the whisk leaves a trail when lifted from the bowl. Remove from the heat and whisk for a further 2 minutes.

2 Sift the flour over the mixture and sprinkle with the biscuit crumbs. Fold in using a large metal spoon. Divide the mixture between the tins and bake in a preheated oven, 180°C (350°F), Gas Mark 4, for 25 minutes or until just firm. Transfer to a wire rack to cool.

3 Halve each cake horizontally and drizzle the layers with half the liqueur. Whisk the mascarpone with the remaining liqueur and icing sugar until smooth. Add the cream and whisk until peaking.

4 Reserve 200 g (7 oz) raspberries and lightly mash the remainder. Sandwich the cake layers together with the mashed raspberries and a little of the cream mixture. Spread the remainder over the top and sides. Scatter with the reserved berries and serve dusted with icing sugar.

Apricot frangipane cake

This cake makes a fabulous gift when it's wrapped in ribbon-tied baking parchment. Cranberries are apt for the festive season, but can be left out at other times of the year.

PREPARATION TIME: 45 minutes

COOKING TIME: about 50 minutes

SERVES 10

175 g (6 oz) unsalted butter, softened

175 g (6 oz) golden caster sugar

3 eggs

100 g (3½ oz) self-raising flour

175 g (6 oz) ground almonds

250 g (8 oz) ready-to-eat dried apricots

5 tablespoons smooth apricot jam

2 tablespoons brandy or almond liqueur

250 g (8 oz) white almond paste

100 g (3½ oz) whole sweet almonds

25 g (1 oz) dried cranberries

Glacé Icing (see page 16)

1 Grease and line the base and sides of an 18 cm (7 inch) round cake tin. Grease the paper. Put the butter, sugar, eggs, flour and ground almonds in a bowl and beat until smooth and creamy. Roughly chop the apricots and stir in 150 g (5 oz).

2 Turn the mixture into the tin, level the surface and bake in a preheated oven, 160°C (325°F), Gas Mark 3, for 50 minutes or until just firm and a skewer inserted into the centre comes out clean. Transfer to a wire rack to cool.

3 Measure the circumference of the cake with a piece of string. Melt the jam with the liqueur in a small saucepan until smooth. Brush a little glaze over the top and sides of the cake. Roll out the almond paste and trim to a strip the length of the string and 1 cm (½ inch) deeper than the cake. Roll up the paste and unroll it around the sides of the cake.

4 Scatter with the remaining apricots, nuts and cranberries. Brush with the remaining glaze and scribble with icing.

Kringle
This recipe is a simplified version of a traditional, sweet Danish bread: mildly spiced, fruity and baked in a pretzel shape. If liked, drizzle the surface of the cooled bread with glacé icing.

PREPARATION TIME: 25 minutes, plus proving

COOKING TIME: 30 minutes

SERVES 10

2 teaspoons easy-blend dried yeast

75 g (3 oz) caster sugar, plus 1 teaspoon

200 ml (7 fl oz) hand-hot milk

400 g (13 oz) strong bread flour

crushed seeds of 15 cardamom pods

1 teaspoon ground mixed spice

1 egg, beaten, plus extra to glaze

75 g (3 oz) salted butter, melted

75 g (3 oz) sultanas

75 g (3 oz) blanched almonds, chopped

2 tablespoons icing sugar

1 Stir the yeast and 1 teaspoon sugar into the milk in a small bowl and leave to stand for 10 minutes or until frothy. Mix the flour with the spices and remaining sugar. Add the egg, butter and yeasted milk and mix to a dough.

2 Turn out on to a floured surface and knead gently for 10 minutes until smooth and elastic. Put in an oiled bowl, cover with clingfilm and leave to rise for about 1 hour or until doubled in size.

3 Knock back the dough (see page 12) and roll it out on a floured surface to a 45 x 15 cm (18 x 6 inch) rectangle. Scatter with the sultanas and all but 15 g (½ oz) of the almonds and roll up. Transfer to a greased baking sheet, curving into a knotted shape. Cover loosely with oiled clingfilm and leave to rise for about 45 minutes or until doubled in size.

4 Brush the surface with beaten egg and dust with icing sugar. Scatter with the reserved nuts and bake in a preheated oven, 190°C (375°F), Gas Mark 5, for 30 minutes or until golden. Cool on a wire rack.

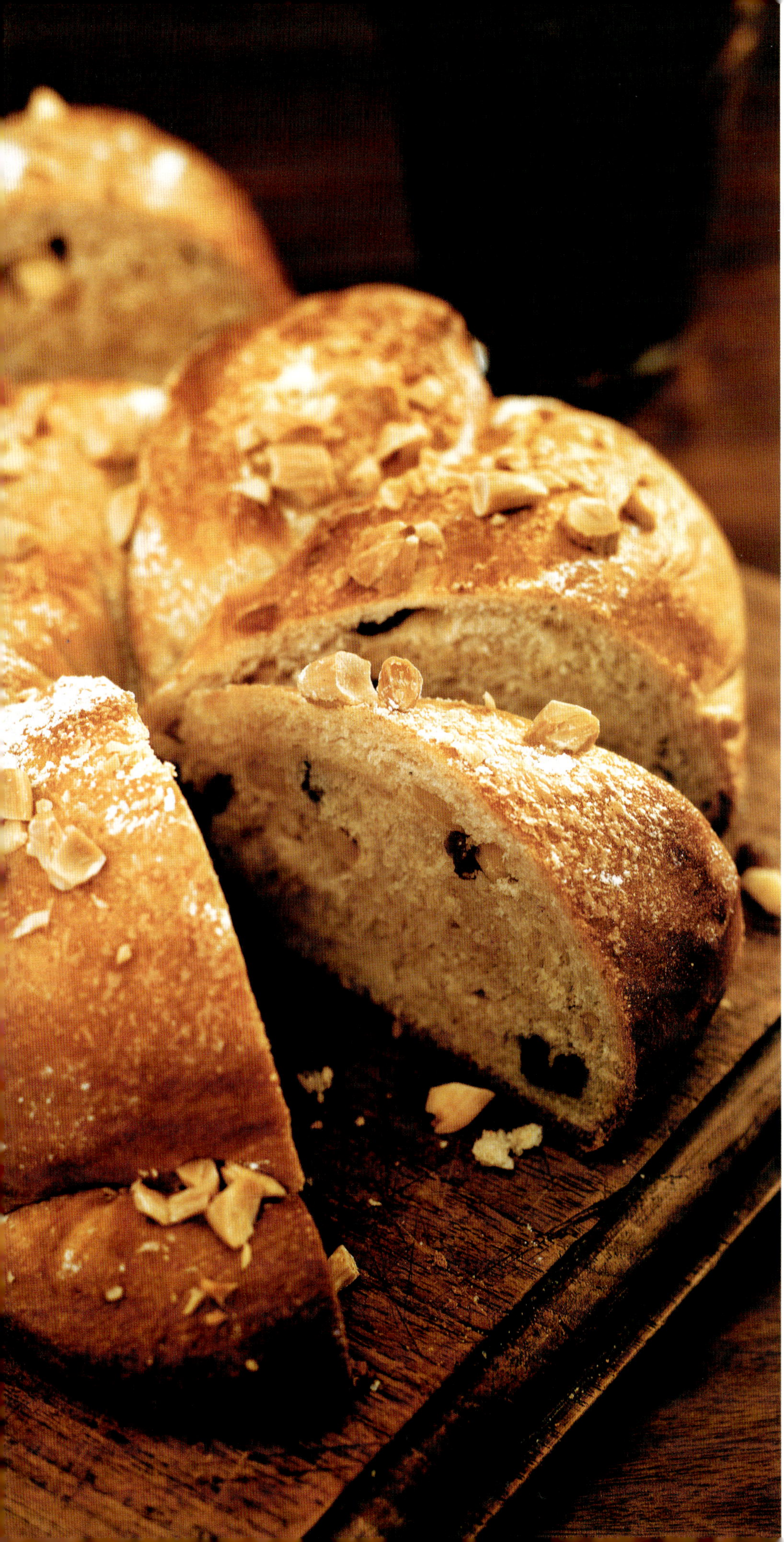

Kringle

Index

Acknowledgements

Photography: © **Octopus Publishing Group Ltd** / Stephen Conroy

Executive Editor Sarah Ford

Editor Fiona Robertson

Deputy Art Director Geoff Fennell

Designer Geoff Borin

Senior Production Controller Manjit Sihra

Photographer Stephen Conroy

Food Stylist Joanna Farrow

Props Stylist Rachel Jukes